GO JOE!

A Journey of Two Hearts

A MEMOIR

JANE P. BAVOSO

Dedicated to Joe's Babies
Jack, Kieran, Julia, Luke, Nora, and Hannah

Go Joe! A Journey of Two Hearts

©2022 Jane P. Bavoso

print ISBN: 978-1-66782-801-5

ebook ISBN: 978-1-66782-802-2

CONTENTS

PREFACE

It has taken me ten years to author this book. It seems like a long time since I know this story well.

When I began, I was faced with many challenges. First, and most important, was that I had to learn how to write. I had to learn how to get my story down on paper, how to keep the interest of the reader, how to best get across the emotional toll it took on our family.

I was encouraged by my long-time friend, Barbara Kaufmann. She insisted I join a writing group with her. I hesitantly agreed and now I thank her for giving me the push I needed.

Mary Haughey was the leader of the first group I joined. An older woman, with years of writing experience under her belt, Mary could size up a person as soon as they walked into the room. She pegged me immediately. I was the one who looked like a deer caught in headlights.

Nervous, and very intimidated, I introduced myself and revealed the reason I was there. I wanted to write a memoir about my husband's experience of receiving two heart transplants. Later, after Mary and I had formed a friendship, she told me, "I knew you were a keeper, Jane, the moment you walked into the room." Mary was encouraging and caring to all her students, cheering every small and big accomplishment.

We lost her a few years back, but I know she is proud of me for finally completing my project. Thank you, Mary, sincerely.

Don Allen took over Mary's classes. Don challenges his writers, motivating them to dig deeper and to take more chances. He took me under his wing and was kind enough to read this book from cover to cover. He always encouraged me, pushing me to reveal more of myself in the story. It was difficult at times, but Don never gave up on me.

Jim McDonald, another fellow writer, is a lover of words. He also was gracious enough to read my manuscript. He would often suggest a different word or phrase to replace the one I had written. He was usually correct.

Jane Waterhouse was my gift. A published writer of mysteries, she read my book as a favor to my son, with whom she had a working relationship. She was gracious and kind, sending me back the manuscript with her own penciled suggestions. She encouraged me to "Get the book published, Jane. It's a story that needs to be shared."

I am never good at picking titles. I can write a three-page story but the choosing of a title always stymies me. I struggled with finding one for this book.

I discovered that Hemingway had pages of potential titles for many of his novels; one of which turned out to be A Farewell to Arms. I knew I was in good company.

I followed Mr. Hemingway's lead. I wrote down lots of titles. I tried to think of something to catch the eye of a reader. But I kept going back to one word in the story, Journey. That was the word Joe always used when describing what he was going through. He always referred to it as his journey. So, who was I to argue with the hero of the book?

"A Journey of Two Hearts" came to me one restless night. It seemed so perfect. Not catchy or slick but so telling.

This story is the tale of a journey of two hearts. The two hearts Joe was gifted with by generous, caring families, who in their own hour of grief were kind and generous enough to try and help another human in need. But this was also the story of Joe and my heart. Our hearts were entwined since we were teenagers. It is so very rare to find your forever person early in life, but we were lucky in that respect. So here is Joe's story and I guess mine as well. I hope I did it justice. Joe deserves nothing less.

PROLOGUE

As I rode the A train, I looked around at all the people riding with me and I questioned if I blended in or if I looked different from them. I was now in my new routine and my thoughts were drifting from present to past. It was an easy thing to do amid the drone of the subway car rattling along the tracks stopping to let riders off or allow new riders on.

I thought about where I was going and where I had been. So much time had passed, so many things had happened. I questioned whether anyone could tell I was a suburban housewife out of her element a little uncomfortable riding the subway to 168th street. It had been so many years since I last used the New York City transit system. Those were the years I lived and grew up in Brooklyn riding the subway to high school every day; laughing and joking with my friends discussing boys, parties, test scores; probably all in that order of importance to a teenager. Those thoughts made me smile and I remembered the tall, cute boy from so many years ago with a muscular build and dark wavy hair with a curl hanging over his forehead.

One of the things I discovered while riding the subway was that you can smile to yourself. You can sit there with a big grin across your face, and nobody gives you a second glance. Everybody seems to be plugged into some electrical device either singing to music no one else can hear or checking their especially important e-mails or texting their very important messages. So, I smiled, and no one cared or noticed.

I remembered the years, so long ago, when I worked in Manhattan thinking how sophisticated I was wearing my stockings and high heel shoes, going to an office for a day's work.

All these thoughts ran through my mind as the train sped through the tunnel bringing me closer to my destination. I could never have imagined, so many months before, how long this so-called journey would last.

In the beginning the thought of riding the subway never occurred to me; a cab brought me from Penn Station to the front of Columbia Presbyterian Hospital. I felt much more secure with a New York city cab driver dropping me off in front of the large intimidating building. As time wore on, I knew I would need to give up this luxury and join the ranks of the subway riders. Now as I rode smiling to myself, I realized how much I would have missed if I had not decided to ride the train. I would never have seen so many different skin colors or heard so many different languages gathered in one place. I would never have witnessed young men offering pregnant women, elderly women, and handicapped people a seat. I would never have observed mothers with infants in strollers, elementary school children dressed in uniforms all going about their everyday activities, riding the subway. No carpools, no school buses, just the subway to get them to their destination. Such a different lifestyle from what I was accustomed to but here I was becoming one of them. I would never have marveled at the supposedly indifferent New Yorkers who went out of their way to help a perfect stranger. I realized how sheltered I had been living in suburbia for so many years.

Many days as I took this trip to visit my husband, I would think of how I got to this place, this so-called journey that I was on, and my mind always brought me back to 1960 in Brooklyn and the beginning of my life with a boy, who at the time, everyone called Joey.

CHAPTER ONE

THE CALL

The jig was up. There was no more denial or fooling myself that we still had plenty of time. Time had run out. I wanted Joe healthy again and to get our life back, but I also wanted to avoid the road we needed to take to achieve that goal. I was frightened—scared to death, really—but Joe seemed to have enough courage for the both of us. He was anxious to get going; me hesitant.

It was 6:45 p.m., and Joe and I were lingering at the kitchen table after dinner. Joe had spent nine weeks in the hospital following complications from receiving a left ventricular assist device, known as an LVAD, and we were trying to get back to some type of normalcy in our lives. At that point life was almost tranquil and quiet. I was content, and then the phone rang, and everything changed.

I had taken a month off from work when Joe came home, knowing he would need my help until he regained his strength. We spent our days on the back deck, enjoying the warm summer sun. After being in the hospital for so many weeks, all Joe wanted was to be outside. He was an outdoors guy—fishing, golfing, and snapping photos of nature every chance he got. I watched him take his walks back and forth across the deck, determined to get in shape for the transplant. When he was a little steadier, he started walking out in front of the house, first to the next house and back, then he managed two houses, then three, until he could walk down the whole block and back. We ate lunch together and played cards, although neither one of us was much of a card player, and we joked that maybe this was what old, retired people did to amuse themselves. But most of all we just accepted each day as a gift.

The day before the call, Joe had asked me to drive him to the beach. We drove together to Captree State Park on a beautiful late September morning, Joe carrying his camera over his shoulder while I packed the extra batteries for the LVAD that always accompanied us when we left the house. I watched him as he walked in the sand, and I was nervous he might stumble when he crouched behind the sea grass to take a picture of the Robert Moses Causeway. I kept my distance, knowing he would be annoyed if I hovered over him. He got himself back up in a standing position without any trouble, and in my mind, I was yelling kudos for him, proud of his determination to become physically strong again.

When the call came in, the caller ID announced it was Columbia Presbyterian Hospital. I handed Joe the phone and watched the expression on his face change.

"Yes," he answered, "this is Joe Bavoso. Yes, I understand. Sure, we'll leave right away." He hung up the phone, looked over at me, and told me what I had already guessed. "They have a heart for me."

We had prepared for this since Joe came home in July. His bag was packed and sitting by the door of our bedroom, ready to go at a moment's notice. Time was of the essence, and Columbia is not a short hop on a weekday night at 7 p.m. Joe was anxious—not nervous, but in a "let's get this thing done" type of way. He stood on the front porch, pacing, waiting for our daughter and son-in-law's car to pull up to the curb. Before walking outside, Joe ran back into the bedroom to do one last thing.

He had been keeping a journal since receiving the LVAD, trying to keep track of his progress and hoping to keep some order in his now upside-down world. On this day, he wrote:

Thursday, 10/1/09

HELLO OCTOBER!

Up at 8:45—weight 178 + lb

Blood work this a.m.—LabCorp was empty

Jane to work about 11 a.m

I went to town . . . J&R, P.O., hardware store, and deli

Made up "Crossing the Sunset" for Jenny and K.C Also did a photo for Lorraine Callahan of the Brooklyn Bridge and Golden Gate

He added at the bottom of the page, underlined and with an asterisk, big and bold:

*Got "THE CALL" @ 6:45 P.M

MY HEART IS IN

We drove up to Columbia in silence, Joe and I sitting in the back seat holding hands, each engrossed in our own thoughts.

When we pulled open the big glass doors of the hospital, Joe darted ahead, hurrying through the lobby without hesitation, like a man on a mission. He located the right desk and signed himself in. After a few moments we were ushered upstairs, and the next part of the journey began.

CHAPTER TWO

The First Heart

Joe was taken to the seventh floor and put in a private room for monitoring until all was ready for surgery. Our son Peter soon joined us, and the rest of the family was alerted.

Finally, after what seemed like forever, Joe was transferred to a holding area outside the operating room, and we were allowed to accompany him. The four of us stood around making small talk, which wasn't easy under the circumstances, while Joe sat up in bed, looking extremely calm. I commented, "Wow, you look more like a person waiting for a plane to take him on vacation than for a heart transplant." He grinned back at me and replied, "I'm ready to get my life back."

I agreed. "It's going to be so great not to be hooked up to an LVAD. You'll be able to move around without being tethered to a machine."

When it was time for Joe to go, each of us kissed him goodbye and told him we loved him. We watched as his bed was pushed through the big swinging doors of the operating room and with a big smile on his face, he gave us a thumbs up. I never shed a tear or showed him I was frightened, although my stomach was in knots. Joe gave me the courage to be brave, and besides, I was confident that the next time I saw him he would be healthy again, with rosy cheeks and a new heart.

We found the family waiting room and discovered no seats were available, so we decided to go back to the seventh floor. None of us slept much, but we were able to sit for a while between taking turns pacing up and down the hall. With dawn approaching, we made our way back downstairs to find some coffee and see if seats had opened up in the family lounge knowing this is where the doctor would look for us after the surgery was completed. It was still crowded, but we managed to find a few chairs and settled in.

As I sat down, I noticed a young man across the room accompanied by a young woman who had severe physical disabilities. Two doctors were talking to them, and as they spoke, their stress level seemed to increase. The young man and woman walked across the room toward us, and I observed the woman struggling to take each step. She was extremely handicapped, yet she asked for no assistance, nor did she carry a cane or other walking device. The man was in so much distress she was almost carrying him.

The two of them stood in front of us, our seats facing the wall. The young man turned his back to us, and with his head leaning against the wall let out the most heart-wrenching howls of sorrow and pain that I have ever heard. He was inconsolable as his body wracked with sobs. Peter leapt from his seat and offered it to the man, who refused the gesture.

Gossip travels fast, even among strangers, and the story soon unfolded. Because of complications, his wife was transferred from a Brooklyn hospital to Columbia to give birth to their child. The new mother was bleeding out and had received over eighty pints of blood; she was on a ventilator, and hopes of recovery were slim. The newly born baby girl was healthy and perfect. Eventually the new father gathered himself together and, accompanied by his female companion, left the waiting room.

And then came our turn. We saw the doctor enter the room, scan the waiting people, and approach us. I don't remember if he asked our name or just knew who we were by description. We had never met. At the time, Columbia had a team of nine heart transplant surgeons. If you were lucky enough to get called for a new heart, the surgeon on rotation would perform the surgery.

He sat across from Lauren, Marty, and me. On the same couch as the doctor were Peter and his wife, Janine, who had by this time also joined us. The doctor kept tapping his leg nervously, his eyes darting around the room, trying to avoid direct eye contact with any one of us. And then he dropped the bomb.

"We couldn't get the heart to start."

No one reacted. It just didn't compute in our brains. All five of us sat there, staring at this young and obviously nervous doctor. He was fumbling for words.

"This is a very rare occurrence, but sometimes it does happen," he continued.

I still didn't react, questioning if I was hearing him correctly. What was he talking about? There was a 98 percent success rate at Columbia for heart transplants. They touted it on their website, and Joe and I put our trust in everything we had read. All I heard were words that didn't make sense to me.

"I'm sorry. We tried everything, but we couldn't sustain a rhythm. Mr. Bavoso is still alive and hooked up to a BiVAD machine. This is acting as his heart. There's a slight chance the new heart may start beating on its own."

Marty was the first to speak. "How much of a chance?"

"Fifty-fifty."

That didn't sound promising to any of us. I sat there speechless. I could feel my heart racing and my mouth going dry. I had no words. I was in shock, stunned, and in disbelief.

After the doctor left, I gazed up and saw Jenn, Joe's favorite LVAD nurse, coming across the room. Jenn and Joe had formed a special bond, and he spoke of her often during his nine-week stay in the hospital after getting the LVAD. Jenn, along with four other nurses, were specially trained to take care of LVAD patients. She was coming on her shift, heard about Joe, and came to the waiting area to find us. When we told her the transplant had failed, Jenn asked me if I would like her to accompany me to the ICU.

I gladly took her up on her offer and answered yes. It was the first word I had spoken since receiving the news.

We all walked to the ICU together, and when we reached Joe's room, I glanced in, stepped back in shock, and totally fell apart. I didn't recognize Joe. He was filled with so many fluids that his face was distorted, and the number of IV bags, wires, and machines surrounding him made it almost impossible to get near the bed. I finally reacted to the news given to me ten minutes earlier. I cried and screamed. I felt my knees buckle, and I knew I was dropping to the floor—and then I felt an arm go around me, lift me up, and help me to a chair. It was Jenn. She tried to soothe me and offer me words of comfort, but I was incapable of being comforted.

Another nurse who was passing by and heard the commotion walked in the room. She spoke sharply, I guess trying to snap me out of it, as they say. "You can't give up because Joe isn't going to give up. He's alive. This is Columbia. He'll survive this, but you have to be strong for him." She told me she had seen this before, and although Joe would have a tough climb, it was surmountable. After a few minutes I caught my breath, controlled my tears, and managed to calm myself down.

We left the hospital a broken family. We were informed that Joe had been immediately put on a high-priority list for another heart, which indicated to me that the chance of the heart pumping on its own was slim. Joe was under heavy sedation, and they planned on keeping him that way until they found out whether the heart would start. They wanted to give it some time, and while I don't think any of the doctors had any hope of that happening, there are procedures in a large hospital, and this was theirs.

The morning after the failed transplant, I was back at the hospital. I knew nothing had changed, but I needed to be there. I was in the waiting room when I noticed the man from the day before sitting not far from me. His head was bent down either in prayer or just utter despair. I walked quietly over to him and touched him on the shoulder. He looked up at me quizzically.

"I was in the waiting room yesterday," I whispered to him. "I said a prayer for your wife." With tears in his eyes, he softly answered, "Thank you."

For the next eight days I clung to hope. When the doctors finally decided, this heart was never going to start, they closed up Joe's chest, which they had kept open since the surgery, and started to slowly bring him out of sedation. That was our next problem.

After eight days, we all had come to terms with what had happened, but we knew that when Joe opened his eyes, he would think it was just after surgery and would expect to be told his new heart was working fine. I needed to speak with Dr. Donna Mancini, the head of the transplant team.

Dr. Mancini was the first doctor we met at Columbia. She had set Joe up to receive an LVAD and saw him for checkups. She was in charge, and everyone knew it. I don't think she was five feet tall and probably weighed no more than ninety pounds, but when she came into the unit, all the doctors, at every level, almost stood at attention. She called the shots. She never smiled or made small talk. She was all business. On one of our visits, she greeted Joe warmly and commented on how well he looked. Joe presented her with a gift of one of his black and white photographs of the Brooklyn Bridge, and on that day, Dr. Mancini smiled.

I went to Dr. Mancini with my concerns and asked if we should, as a family, inform Joe of the transplant failure, and whether we should have the psychiatrist with us for guidance. Dr. Mancini looked straight at me and said no, she would tell Joe.

I voiced concern again. "But he'll be in shock—he might need his family around him," I protested.

"No," she told me again, in no uncertain terms. "Mrs. Bavoso, we need to wake Joe slowly," she said. "Each time he regains some level of consciousness we will explain it to him until he fully understands. I promise you, he'll be fine."

So I put my trust in Dr. Mancini.

CHAPTER THREE

The Awakening

We had a huge following of Joe's journey. I had been sending out emails to update family and friends. They in turn had forwarded my email to their family and friends asking for prayers and good wishes for Joe. We had hundreds of people following our story, sending out good vibes and hopes for the heart to start, to beat on its own. When Peter sent his own emails, he always ended his updates with the mantra GO JOE. I thought this was a great slogan, so I also started to close each of my updates with that phrase. GO JOE became our rallying cry. People started emailing me back regarding Joe's current situation and ended their emails with GO JOE. Any get well cards or prayer cards I received would also have this slogan either written on the envelope or on the inside. People were reaching out to us from all parts of our life. Family friends asked permission to distribute wristbands with GO JOE printed on them, so we began distributing them to everyone we knew. We mailed them to people around the country who were keeping track of Joe's status and they sent pictures to us showing the band on their wrists. Even the doctors and nurses at Columbia who were caring for Joe wore them.

On the ninth day after the surgery, Joe was able to open his eyes when I spoke to him. He would squeeze my hand and wiggle his toes when I asked.

On the tenth day, when I reached his room, Joe was sitting up in the bed and was off the ventilator. He greeted me with his big smile and said, "Hey, what are you doing here?"

I jokingly answered, "Well, how could I resist visiting a big, strapping man tied to a bed?"

He rolled his eyes in feigned exasperation.

I was ecstatic that Joe was awake and talking but definitely concerned because I knew the questions would now begin. "Joe, did Dr. Mancini explain what happened?"

"Yeah, I understand. But I have a question for you."

"Sure. What is it?"

"What's the plan?"

Joe was a definite type A personality. He needed a plan. And so I explained.

"You're on a high-priority list to receive a new heart. The doctors told me that every heart that's offered to Columbia has your name on it. They're having lots of activity, but they're waiting for the perfect heart, a local heart from the Tri-State area. The quicker they can get the heart to the hospital, the better chance of it pumping on its own. They all seem very positive. Right now it's just a waiting game."

Joe seemed satisfied with that answer. There was a plan. I looked at this man and he amazed me. There was no despair in his eyes, only hope. He was living up to his reputation as my hero. But two days later his strength would be tested again.

I had a good visit with Joe. Although on the BiVAD, a rather cumbersome apparatus, he appeared stronger. Around 5 p.m., it was discovered that his hemoglobin count had dropped from 10 to 6.7. A normal range for men was between 13.5 to 17.5 so Joe was already below normal. They prepared to give Joe two units of blood. Dr. Mancini had been getting ready to transfer Joe out of the ICU to a step-down unit, but that was put on hold.

I went home deflated and spoke with a nurse around 10 p.m. She told me she ordered a sonogram because Joe had a large hematoma on his leg. They thought he may be bleeding internally.

The next day, his hemoglobin count went up a bit. By now they had given him a third unit of blood. The infectious disease doctor was sent in, but there was no sign of infection. They concluded that the high white blood cell count was probably from the pooling of blood in his leg. Dr. Mancini ordered a CT scan. Because of backups in the hospital, it took seven hours for Joe to get this test. At this point, Joe was in so much pain they were giving him Percocet, which didn't seem to be helping. Marty had come to the hospital that evening after work and insisted the nurse give Joe morphine so he could get some relief. After a lot of discussion, the powers above finally agreed.

The next day, as I pulled up to the hospital, Joe called me on my cell. He announced that he was out of the ICU and in a step-down unit. The work now had to start all over again. Joe had to once again be ready for the next transplant. Dave Zemmel, the physical therapist, arrived on the scene. Dave had worked with Joe in May when he received the LVAD and fought pneumonia for nine weeks. Joe was a pretty big guy. He was six feet tall and weighed at this time around 170 pounds. Dave was a slight man; he was lucky if he was five foot six and probably weighed around 140 pounds, but he had the biggest smile and personality around. He and Joe hit it off the moment they met and they became friends. We were thrilled when Dave walked into the room, although I don't think Dave would have allowed another PT to take Joe on as a patient.

"Well, buddy, here we go again," was Dave's greeting to Joe.

"Hey, Dave. Well, I'm glad I'm keeping you employed. Now let's get started so I can get the hell out of this bed."

And so it began. He and Joe understood each other, and Joe responded to every demand Dave made of him. They worked as a team. I was amazed at how this small man could move, maneuver, and sometimes even lift Joe.

His words were always encouraging, and I knew that Dave, on each visit, worked with Joe longer than was required.

They were buddies, sharing stories and jokes while they worked together.

"So, Dave, buy that girlfriend of yours a ring yet?"

"Come on Joe. I'm getting there. It's a big step," Dave answered with a smile and a twinkle in his eye.

They were just like two guys anywhere, out for a beer ribbing each other. I thanked God every day for Dave.

The day after Joe was released from the ICU, he sat up in a chair for two hours. It was a major accomplishment. The next day he walked with the help of Dave, a nurse, and Peter. Because of the apparatus, a team effort was needed. Khristine, one of the nurses on the team, pushed the BiVAD, Peter walked behind Joe with a chair, and Dave walked beside Joe, encouraging him and watching his vitals.

Joe was becoming well-known in the hospital, and there were scores of doctors in and out of the room on a daily basis. Joe was a VP of marketing for his firm, and he always had lots of ideas swirling around in his head. He was determined to come up with a better idea to promote organ donation. A doctor by the name of Schulman was interested in Joe's thoughts, and they had many discussions. He told Joe, "When all this is over and you're back on your feet, I want you to come see me, and we'll discuss some of your ideas."

The next day, Joe walked again and a doctor passing by yelled out, "Hey, Joe Bavoso, everyone knows you! We're looking really hard for a heart for you!" He was becoming a celebrity in the hospital, but that was not the way we wanted him to become famous.

CHAPTER FOUR

REMEMBERING

I learned quickly that when you have a loved one in the ICU or a step-down unit (an intermediate level of care between the ICU and the general medical-surgical ward) you spend a lot of time in the family lounge. There always seems to be something happening in the patient's room, and you're frequently asked to step outside. Sitting there hour after hour gives you lots of time to people watch, pray, reflect on the situation, or just remember. Alone with my thoughts, memories came streaming back, not only the memories of how this journey all began, but more importantly of how we began: the beginning of this friendship, partnership, and love affair that had begun so many years before. It seems that wherever you go, you either meet someone who came from Brooklyn, once lived in Brooklyn, visited Brooklyn, or drove through Brooklyn. It was a great place to grow up in the fifties and sixties, and that's where Joe and I started our life together.

Dressed in my navy-blue parochial school uniform, I first spotted him while I waited for the city bus. He would come bounding across the street, heading for the subway on his way to high school. I was turning thirteen and in the eighth grade; he was a freshman. He was tall with dark slicked-down hair, neatly dressed in khakis and a short-sleeved button-down shirt, his books tucked under his arm and his head cocked to one side, like he was deep in concentration. He always walked quickly past me, never giving me a glance, running down the subway steps to catch his train.

I didn't know him, had never uttered a word to him or he to me, and yet each time I saw him, my heart fluttered a bit. Finally, a year later, we met. Joe didn't disappoint. His smile was infectious, his demeanor easygoing. Our conversation was effortless, the banter flowing back and forth. I was falling fast and hoped the same was happening to him, but then I discovered that Joe had a crush on someone else.

And not just someone else - one of my best friends.

My teenage heart was broken, but in public I was stoic. If nothing else, we had formed a strong friendship—so strong, in fact, that I tried to help him secure the affection of my friend, all the while hoping that he would take off his blinders and see me. After she rejected him, I was there to listen and to offer comfort. We took long walks together, sharing our interests and dreams.

Joe was the oldest of six in a working-class family. He was expected to pull his own weight, so he always had an after-school job and many times was responsible for his five siblings. He was sure of himself—not cocky, just confident in his decisions. He loved art and took classes; he loved music and played the drums in a band. And in time, he felt comfortable enough with me to share his disappointments.

"You know, I made the football team at school," he told me one night.

"Wow, that's great!" I replied.

"Nah, it's not great. My mother found out and flipped out."

"Why?" I asked?

"I was born with a stupid heart murmur. I'm not supposed to play sports. When she found out, she called the school, and so that's the end of my sports career."

"I'm really sorry. I know how much you love football."

"I mean, look at me," Joe replied, "Do I look like I can't play football?" I had to admit he looked pretty healthy to me, all six feet of him and a darn good build at the age of fifteen. "I'm really pissed about the whole thing."

"That's okay," I said, "you'll find something else you're good at that you like."

However, there was no consoling him that night. "Do you realize that I won't be able to become a cop or join the Coast Guard?"

I tried to be as sympathetic as a fourteen-year-old could be. "I'm really, really sorry, but you have lots of time to make some other choices."

And then it happened. The blinders came off, and in March 1962, we became a couple. He was kind, respectful, and affectionate, everything you would want in a boyfriend. As happy as I was to be with Joe, I was also cautious. I had been around too many teenage girls who were always falling in love and getting their hearts broken. I took that word very seriously and in no uncertain terms warned Joe never to use it. I think he was a little taken aback.

"Who knows what love is?" I told him. "Certainly not me, and definitely not you." And so the word was never spoken.

On my sixteenth birthday, after we had been going steady for fifteen months, Joe presented me with a gift. At that time, gold charm bracelets were in style. A charm would be added to the bracelet for every major event in your life. My sister had given me the bracelet as a gift, three years before, when I was a bridesmaid in her bridal party. I excitedly opened the small box Joe handed to me. He immediately saw the surprise on my face. In the box was a charm in the shape of a stop sign with the words "I'll Never Stop Loving You" etched on it.

Even at seventeen, Joe was never at a loss for words. He quickly quipped, "Well, I couldn't find one that said, I'll Never Stop Liking You."

I attached the charm to the bracelet.

At eighteen, I started questioning our relationship. I had been with Joe since three months before my fifteenth birthday. I was now working in the city, meeting lots of new people.

"Suppose he's not the one for me," I said to myself. "Suppose I end up committing myself to the wrong person." And so I approached him with a plan.

"We should take a break," I told him one night. "It's not a breakup, just a break," I continued. I suggested a four-week breather.

Dumbfounded, he agreed and offered no argument. So for one month, I was single. Every weekend took my friends and me to a scene I had thought I might be missing out on. Eighteen was the drinking age at the time, so on a Friday night I would accompany friends to a bar to dance, listen to music and of course scout out the guys. It didn't take me long to realize no one could compare to the boyfriend I already had.

After the four weeks were up, there were no apologies, accusations, pointing of fingers, or I-told-you-sos. We just seemed to meld together again as easily as we had come together in the beginning. Neither one of us could remember who said the words "I love you" first. It didn't really matter: those words flowed easily between the two of us throughout the rest of our life together.

After arguments, disagreements, stomping of feet, and sometimes tears, those words always found their way out of our mouths. It's probably what saved us numerous times. There was never a telephone conversation that didn't end with "I love you," a goodnight kiss that wasn't sealed with those words, or a goodbye hug that didn't include them. It became as natural to us as waving goodbye to a friend.

My thoughts were interrupted when I looked up and saw the physically handicapped woman who I had noticed a few days before coming towards me. I hadn't seen her since that awful morning. When she reached me, I looked up. She was the first to speak.

"I want to thank you."

"For what?"

"My cousin's husband, Eli, told me you approached him and told him you said a prayer for his wife."

"I did. I was there that morning."

"Eli was so very touched by your gesture of caring."

She introduced herself as Elizabeth and explained that Eli and her cousin, also named Elizabeth, had two other children at home. Eli was totally devastated and almost on the brink of a nervous breakdown. Although the large family had stepped in to care for the children, he was beyond distraught. His wife was on a ventilator and the prognosis wasn't good.

"Your simple act has given him some hope," she said, "He was deeply touched by the kindness of a stranger."

She inquired as to why I was at the hospital. I told her my story.

"What's your husband's name and his mother's name?" she asked.

"Joe, and his mother's name was Rita."

Elizabeth and her family belonged to a Jewish community, and she explained that when they included someone in prayer, the mother's name of the person they are praying for is always mentioned.

"From now on," Elizabeth promised, "Joe, son of Rita, will be included in our daily prayers."

After that encounter, every time I walked into the family lounge and saw the circle of bearded men sitting in a corner of the room with prayer shawls draped over their shoulders, heads bobbing in prayer, reading from their sacred books, I knew that "Joe, son of Rita," was being prayed for.

Over the next few months, Elizabeth proved to be a comfort, companion, and watchful eye. At times, I would pass her in the hall and she would tell me that she had sat with Joe for a while. "I didn't want him to be alone until you got here. He slept and I prayed."

As I got to know Elizabeth a little better, she shared with me that she was a speech pathologist who worked with children. This amazing woman who had so many struggles of her own had dedicated her life to helping children overcome their struggles. She was now determined to help her cousin get well again. When Joe managed to come off the ventilator, she used him as an example for her cousin, who was having a difficult time being weaned from the machine.

On another day, she brought a young couple to Joe's room and introduced them. The young man was facing the possibility of receiving an LVAD, which might eventually lead to a heart transplant. Elizabeth thought Joe was the best person for them to meet and so Joe spoke with the couple for several minutes.

"What happened to me won't happen to you," Joe reassured them as they looked a little anxiously at the BiVAD machine. "This was a really rare occurrence, just bad luck. But I'm on a high-priority list. I'm going to get another heart, and when I do, I'll have my life back. I won't give up, and neither can you. You're half my age. If I can do this, so can you. You have your whole life ahead. Life is too precious not to fight for."

Late one afternoon, Elizabeth stopped by Joe's room before departing for home. "Today is a very holy day on the Hebrew calendar," she told us as she stood in the doorway. "Tonight, Joe, you will be included in our prayers."

One small, kind gesture brought Joe into a circle of love and prayer from total strangers. Elizabeth and Joe were very different, but also very much alike. They both took the challenges life threw at them and faced them head on.

CHAPTER FIVE

WAITING

Each day as I traveled to the hospital, I had high hopes. Joe was working with Dave to get stronger in anticipation of his next heart transplant. I would enter the hospital thinking that maybe today would be the day—maybe today we would get our second chance. It's funny, I always thought of it as *we*, not *he*. We were in this together. I was at Columbia seven days a week. I was Joe's connection with the outside world. I was the bearer of family news.

"Hannah's taking some steps now," I would tell him. "Jack's doing well in first grade. He's very proud of his new reading skills. Julia and Kieran are enjoying preschool, and the twins are now in the Twos Program-can you believe that?"

"The Twos Program!"

"Soon they'll go from the cradle right into school!"

We laughed together about that. Our kids never went to nursery school, much less a Twos Program.

"You know," I would continue, "they all ask for you every day. *When is Papa coming home?* That's all they ask me."

And then I would see the sadness in Joe's eyes.

"God, I really miss them," he would tell me. I knew he did, and I also knew I had to reassure him often that the children were not forgetting him. I told him they prayed for him each night before they went to sleep and that

Kieran, our five-year-old grandson wouldn't let anyone else sit in Papa's chair at the table when we had dinner together each Sunday.

"Poppy," Kieran would say to his paternal grandfather, "don't forget that's Papa's chair when he comes home."

And Frank would always answer, "Don't worry, Kieran, when Papa comes home I'll give him back his seat at the table." And then Frank would lead us in grace and always include a prayer for Joe.

It was difficult for Joe when his heart started to deteriorate. He had no energy or strength to spare. He couldn't roll around on the floor with the children or toss them up in the air to shrieks of laughter. He would sit on the couch and hold Hannah, our youngest grandbaby in his lap. Joe would rock her in his arms for hours.

After our Sunday night family dinner at Lauren's, Joe would come home depressed.

"I can't even play with the kids like I used to. Look at Frank. He's sixteen years older than me, and he's giving them piggyback rides up the stairs to bed." He was right. Frank was as strong as a bull and Joe was, quite frankly, jealous. Who could blame him?

After Joe received the LVAD, he would hold onto the children for as long as they would sit still. I was always nervous, afraid that one of them would touch the wires or buttons on the device. The LVAD was keeping Joe alive until he got his transplant, so I was always hovering around when the kids were near it. This drove Joe crazy. He would tell me in no uncertain terms, "It's okay. Stop worrying—they're not going to touch anything."

But worry I did. He just wanted things to be as they were before.

I know he waited for me to show up every day at the hospital, but I was certain a new face, a different visitor, was a big treat. Columbia was not an easy trip for any of our family or friends, but we were lucky that over the extended amount of time Joe spent there, some hearty souls, God bless them, made the effort.

On one such day I looked up to see Dr. Marzo and Dr. Germano entering the room. They were Joe's cardiologist and electrophysiologist from Winthrop Hospital in Mineola on Long Island who had taken care of him for the past eight years. They were both wonderful doctors and good people, so I shouldn't have been too surprised. Joe's face lit up when he spotted them. He welcomed them like old friends, which in fact they had become. They chatted, laughed, and discussed photography, just as they always did when Joe was their patient. I'm sure they also checked out the BiVAD Joe was hooked up to. You didn't get to see that type of equipment at Winthrop.

We met Dr. Kevin Marzo in 2001. Joe had gone for a simple stress test ordered by Dr. Robert Curran, our primary care physician, as part of his annual physical. Joe was fifty-five years old.

On an autumn day in October, the phone rang at work, and when I answered, I was surprised to hear Joe's voice on the other end, sounding rather concerned. "You're not going to believe this," he stammered into the phone. "I just got a call from the doctor who administered the stress test. He wants to see me right away. He thinks I had a heart attack."

"There must be some mistake," I said.

"How," he continued, "could I have suffered a heart attack? I never felt any pain, and I feel fine. God Almighty, I go to the gym four days a week!"

I knew Joe was frightened, and in his present state of mind there were really no words I could offer to console or comfort him.

"I'll meet you at the doctor's office," I offered.

"No, no," he told me. "I'm okay. I'll see you at home after I see the doctor."

When Joe walked into the house, he was more agitated than earlier. The doctor had made an error. He hadn't suffered a heart attack after all, but something was definitely wrong, and more tests had been ordered.

That's when our relationship with Dr. Marzo began. He was highly recommended to perform the angiogram to rule out any blockages to the heart. After the test, we got the good news that all Joe's arteries were clear.

We were feeling pretty good until Dr. Marzo entered the room. He was kind and caring and I liked him right away. He informed us that although there was no blockage, the tests indicated that Joe had a weakened heart muscle. Dr. Marzo must have seen the look of panic on my face because I felt an arm go around my shoulder and heard Dr. Marzo's reassuring words, "We can treat this with medication."

The next step was an intracardiac electrophysiology test, or EPS, which tests how well the heart's electrical signals are working and checks for abnormal heart rhythms. Joe passed that test too.

They couldn't sustain an arrhythmia. Joe's heart kept going back to normal rhythm on its own. This information was given to me by a short, burly, bearded Physician's Assistant. He talked and joked with all the patients in the absence of the electrophysiologist who administered the test. I asked the PA if I could speak with the doctor. The PA gave me a small, sympathetic smile and said, "Oh, you'll never see him. If the test is okay, he doesn't bother to talk to the patient or family."

This was the start of our long ordeal dealing with different doctors and their personalities. Never being good at hiding my feelings, I think the PA took pity on me after seeing me in some distress. I will never forget his words: "Honey, believe me, he's not going to die tonight. You've been here all day; go home, relax, have something to eat. He won't be released until nine. Come back then."

I hesitated and again was told in no uncertain terms to go home. And so I did. I called our family and watched the clock until I could return to the hospital. I got there at exactly 9 p.m. and was greeted with "Where have you been?" by the woman at the desk. "Where've I been? Home. I was told to go home and come back at nine."

"Well, we've been paging you. Your husband's been ready for release, but we couldn't find you. He told us you would never leave the hospital without him."

Of course, it never dawned on anybody to call me at home. When I got Joe in the car, he was livid. Not one to have much patience, he was more than annoyed that I had left the hospital, even though I explained what the PA had instructed me to do. It was a tense and quiet ride home. I often thought about that incident. Maybe Joe felt I had abandoned him. I tried, in all the long months that followed, to never make him feel that way again.

CHAPTER SIX

Moving Forward

It took us a while before we found our way back to Dr. Marzo. Having never needed a heart doctor before, Joe decided to retain the cardiologist who had administered the stress test. It was a decision that we often disagreed on because after every appointment Joe would come home annoyed.

"This guy has absolutely no personality," he would complain.

"Well, if you don't like him, you should find someone else."

"Nah, I guess he's okay," was Joe's standard reply.

I never understood his thinking. Joe connected with people almost immediately, and he thought it important to have a good relationship with a doctor. Joe was a doctor's delight, keeping track of his overall health and following the doctor's suggestions and recommendations. If a test could keep him healthy, he was willing to take it. When it was suggested that we both have a colonoscopy, Joe was the first one to sign up.

"Better to be safe than sorry," he would tell me when I turned up my nose at the unpleasant procedure.

When Joe came home from his initial appointment with the gastroenterologist who would be performing the test, he greeted me with "You're not going to believe what happened," stifling a chuckle.

"I'm almost afraid to ask."

"I was waiting in the exam room, and the doctor walked in. I look at him and tell him, 'Hey, I know you!' So he looks a little startled and asks me, 'Oh yeah? From where?' From the cover of *The Long Island Fisherman*."

Joe was an avid fisherman, and *The Long Island Fisherman* arrived in our mailbox every week. Dr. Boshnack had been featured on the cover of the publication a few days before after he caught a record-breaking striped bass.

"So" Joe recounted, "he laughs, runs out the door into the waiting area yelling to his staff, 'Hey, I found a fan,' and then comes running back into the exam room with the paper in his hand. We talked about fishing and our favorite spots. He's a really nice guy."

That was Joe's personality, so it was understandable that not connecting with this cardiologist really irked him.

After another visit to the heart doctor, Joe came home more agitated than usual.

"What's wrong now?" I asked.

"He told me that although I don't qualify for a defibrillator now, and the insurance company wouldn't pay for it, it would still be a good idea to have one implanted. I asked him how I could do that. He said I could pay for it myself. It costs $30,000!"

I looked at Joe disbelieving. "He really didn't say that to you, did he?"

"Oh yes, he did."

"That's insane. How could we possibly do that?"

And then Joe said something to me that stopped me in my tracks. "Jane, this is my life we're talking about. You want to put a price on my life?"

"Joe," I said as gently as I could, "I think it's time to find another doctor."

The decision was taken out of Joe's hands when he received a call from the cardiologist's office informing him that the doctor was no longer with the practice and inquiring if he would like to make his appointment with someone else. I looked at Joe and said, "I think you should call Dr. Marzo's office. I really liked him, and he has a great reputation."

Joe agreed. It was one of the best decisions he ever made.

I accompanied Joe on his initial visit to Dr. Marzo. When Dr. Marzo entered the examining room, he greeted us with a smile and a handshake like a longtime friend. He was a nice-looking man, small in stature. After shaking our hands, he jumped up on a cabinet along the wall and while chatting with us swung his legs back and forth, like a kid pumping himself on a swing. It was all so casual. He discussed Joe's heart issues, explaining that the condition was called cardiomyopathy and was caused by one of three things: a heart attack, which was ruled out; alcoholism, which didn't apply to Joe; or a virus. The virus shows up as the flu, hits the heart and causes damage, and then leaves the body. The sick person gets better without feeling any after-effects, except the heart is left damaged. There was no timeframe on when this could have happened. It didn't really matter—the damage was done. Dr. Marzo agreed that a defibrillator might be needed sometime in the future, but not right now. For now, Joe would be put on a regimen of medications that hopefully would help strengthen his heart. He would be monitored closely.

We knew we had found the right guy.

CHAPTER SEVEN

STILL WAITING

I've always had an intense dislike of hospitals. I loathe the smell of antiseptics and ammonia when I walk through the doors. I hate the sterile feel, the carts being wheeled around carrying medications and machinery. I have an aversion to the shuffling of patients lying on gurneys from one room to another. So it was ironic to me that for the past nine years I had spent so much time in hospitals.

Each morning on my trip to Columbia, the screeching of the brakes on the train assaulted my ears and sent shivers up my spine. It reminded me of nails on a blackboard, and I often said to myself, "I should wear earbuds like everyone else to muffle out the sound." But I knew I never would. I liked to be aware of my surroundings and wearing earbuds in a public place would be more stressful.

I would exit the train and breathe in the mixed smells of body odor, garbage, and too much cologne splashed on young executives in training, and I would then hurriedly climb the long staircase to escape the dingy area and sometimes be met by the soft touch of a spring shower. Umbrellas of all colors and designs passed by, but on some days I would refuse to open mine. The dampening of my hair and skin felt like a cleansing after the long ride on the dirty subway.

The food trucks would be lined up, offering every variety of beverage or edible item. Tea and coffee for the traditionalist, power drinks for the health-conscious, juice slushies for the under twenty-five crowd. You could have anything from a bagel to a burrito to a salted pretzel or the good old standard of bacon, cheese, and egg on a roll. It was all there for the asking, every smell more enticing than the last. However, I never stopped at the trucks. The lines were always long, lots of people waiting for their morning fix. I was always anxious to get to Joe's room as quickly as possible.

As I walked briskly along the street, I watched a variety of vehicles scrambling for parking spaces or lining up to wait at a red light. I heard the cars, buses, trucks, and taxis impatiently blowing their horns at strolling pedestrians or vehicles blocking their way. It was a familiar sound of the city that by now I had become accustomed to. I would cross the busy thoroughfare and approach the hospital, putting my hand out to grab the cold steel handle that would open the big glass door. Once inside, the sights and sounds would change. There would be rolling carts, clanging bells and alarms, the sound of running feet on tile floors. All those noises would send shivers up my spine, reminding me that there was always a crisis somewhere in the hospital, and I would pray that Joe would be spared that day.

I would hesitate for a moment and take a deep breath. I was torn. I didn't want to walk into that hospital because I was always walking into the unknown, and yet I was eager to get to Joe's room to see him and hold his hand. Finally, I would pull open the door and enter my world of chaos and uncertainty. If I was lucky, Paris would be there. Paris was the security guard at the front desk.

He was a tall, thin man dressed in a blue blazer, tie, and button-down shirt with a big smile on his face and a name badge attached to his lapel. On some days, when the line of visitors was extremely long, I would hear my name called out and see an arm waving me to the front of the line. When I reached the desk, Paris would hand me my pass, wish me a good day, and tell me that he was praying for both me and "Mr. B."

On one such day, Paris told me, "Mrs. B., I left something for you in your husband's room. I put it on his table next to the bed."

When I entered the room, I saw a small guardian angel pin exactly where Paris told me he left it. Later, I took a short break from sitting with Joe and went downstairs to the lobby to thank Paris for the gift. "You're very welcome, Mrs. B. I gave you the gift of an angel because you are an angel." I wore that pin religiously every day. I don't think Paris ever knew that on some days he was the only ray of sunshine in my life.

* * *

The doctors were constantly focusing on Joe's EF, or ejection fraction. A normal heart pumps just over half the heart's volume of blood with each beat—a normal EF is 55 to 75 percent. Joe's was pumping at around 25 percent. We had limited his salt intake to a minimum. I purchased cookbooks that were written especially for patients suffering from heart failure. I tried my best to make interesting and tasty meals that were heart healthy. Joe kept up an exercise program and limited his fluid intake. As I mentioned before, he was a very compliant patient because he knew the risks and ramifications of noncompliance.

Joe did pretty well under Dr. Marzo's guidance. He was put on a drug called Coreg, which was to help strengthen the heart and control AFib, and then on Altace, which was also a heart-strengthening drug. One of the side effects was fatigue. Joe was an active guy. He was still working every day, fishing on his boat every weekend, golfing with a group of buddies once a month, and trying to get a photography business started. He went from being an amateur photographer to a semi-professional one. We worked together exhibiting his photographs in art shows on Long Island, and he was beginning to make a name for himself. We quickly learned that outdoor art shows are a lot of work. They demand physical labor, and I was always amazed at how Joe managed to do all the heavy lifting that was required. He would joke and tell me that he had to figure out a better way to sell his photographs.

"After all," he would quip, "we're not getting any younger. We can't do this forever."

I also knew that Joe was a people person, and I would listen to him as he engaged in conversation with potential buyers regarding the camera, lenses, and techniques he used.

Dr. Marzo tried slowly to increase the dosage of the drugs, but they left Joe so exhausted he was becoming depressed. After working all week, he had little or no energy to do anything else. One time, we had dinner plans with friends. He was looking forward to the evening, but by five o'clock he looked at me and said, "I can't go out to dinner. I feel awful, I'm so exhausted I can hardly move. You're going to have to cancel."

That was the first time in our lives that we cancelled plans that late. I was a little embarrassed, but as I watched Joe, I knew he would never have been able to get through the evening. We also knew that Dr. Marzo would have to lower the dosage of the drugs. He did just that, and it worked for a while, until he finally told us it was time to have a consultation with the electrophysiologist.

We made an appointment to see Dr. Joseph Germano, who was a member of Dr. Marzo's medical team. When Dr. Germano walked into the exam room, I did a double-take. At first I thought, *Oh, this must be the doctor's PA.* Dr. Germano looked too young to be the electrophysiologist. I was wrong.

Dr. Germano, just like his counterpart, greeted us warmly with a big smile and friendly handshake. He explained to us what a defibrillator is, how it works, and the reasons for implanting one. He also told us that he took the implanting of a defibrillator very seriously. "Putting in a defibrillator alters your lifestyle, but it will also save your life," he told us during our first meeting. Before putting in the device, he wanted another doctor's opinion. He and Dr. Marzo both agreed that Joe should have an MRI of his heart and that it should not be done at Winthrop but at St. Francis Hospital. According to them, that's where the best doctor in the country was when it came to reading the results. "Let's see if he agrees with us," said Dr. Germano.

On our ride home, I mentioned to Joe how young the electrophysi-ologist was. "I think I'd feel a little better if he had a few strands of gray in his hair." Joe didn't flinch. "Not me. I like the young doctors. They're up on the newest procedures. I have full confidence in him."

So Joe made the appointment and went alone for the MRI. Although I offered to accompany him, I got the usual reply: "I'll be fine. I can go by myself."

The next visit with Dr. Germano confirmed the decision to put in the device. The doctor at St. Francis had agreed it should be done. I felt a little panic in my chest. Medication was one thing, but a device was another. I looked at this very young doctor, who I had determined was younger than my two children and asked him a question that was weighing on my mind. "How many of these devices have you implanted?"

He smiled at me and said, "About five hundred."

I decided he was qualified.

The defibrillator was implanted, and Joe came home with a sore chest and instructions not to raise his arm for a few days. He also came home with a tracking monitor that would be placed next to our bed. Joe was taught how to interrogate his heart, and the results would be sent directly to the doctor's office. The nurse would read it every day and make notes of any changes in Joe's heart rhythm. This was a whole new lifestyle for us, and the monitor was a constant reminder that life was not the same anymore. When friends and family asked Joe how he felt about having this device, his answer was always the same: "It's like having a gun in a bad neighborhood. You hope you don't have to use it, but you're sure glad you have it if you do."

I called these Joe's idioms. He always seemed to have one to fit every occasion. All was well for fifteen months—and then everything started to go downhill.

CHAPTER EIGHT

THE SLIPPERY SLOPE

We were told that 99 percent of the time, a defibrillator never fires. I have to admit, I did sleep better. I felt Joe was safe now with this machine keeping his heart in rhythm. Many times before the device was implanted, I would lay next to Joe at night and listen to his breathing, holding my own breath when at times it seemed like Joe was holding his. Then I would hear his next breath come, and I could relax for a moment.

We felt so confident that in June we decided to take a drive to Virginia for a long weekend. We loved Old Town Alexandria. Once we parked the car at the hotel, we walked what seemed like miles for the next three days, and Joe always had his camera hanging off his shoulder. The weather was beautiful, and the flowers were blooming. Cobblestone streets and brightly colored front doors on the row houses were a photographer's delight and afforded Joe lots of photo opportunities. He did great, never seeming to tire after our long walks.

We both also loved Montauk and had been going out to the East End, first for long weekends, and then for a full week every September for the past twenty-five years. We always went the week of our anniversary and celebrated each year by watching the sun set over Fort Pond Bay. Montauk is also a photographer's dream, and Joe took full advantage of not only the sunsets but the sunrises, getting up early a few times a week and trudging out to the Point in the predawn hours. He loved to capture the sun rising over the lighthouse, its rays reflecting on the water. Most of Joe's photographs were of the East End, and when we participated in the Montauk Art Show held in August each year, he always did very well selling his photographs.

Because Joe was able to take more time off from his job than I was from mine, he would often go out to Montauk alone. He had a friend at work who owned a house out there, and she encouraged Joe to take advantage of her offer to stay overnight, which he finally did. The morning after he got to Montauk, he called me. We chatted about the weather, where he ate dinner, if he got any good shots, and what time he would be home.

But then the conversation grew serious.

"Something weird happened last night," he told me.

"What'd you mean something weird?"

"Something woke me up. It startled me, but I can't tell you what it was. I thought maybe a deer went by the house and woke me up. I can't explain it. It was just a weird feeling."

Joe was not one to startle easily, so I was surprised by the tone in his voice. "Well, it really is quiet where you are, so even a deer walking by would probably sound loud."

"Yeah, it must have been a deer," he answered, not too convincingly.

When he got home, he interrogated his heart and sent the results over to Dr. Marzo's office.

A nurse called after reading the results.

"Hi, Mr. Bavoso. This is Trish from Dr. Marzo's office. I just read your read out. You had an incident. Did you feel anything?"

"When did it happen?" asked Joe.

"Last night. Well, early this morning. I can give you the exact time: 2:43 a.m."

"Something woke me up, but I couldn't figure out what it was. I can't say I felt anything, but something did feel strange. I was telling my wife about it this morning."

"Your device fired. It was a mild shock. Dr. Marzo wants you to come into the office, and we'll interrogate it here. You might need a few adjustments."

"Wow, I didn't expect that. I've had it for fifteen months, and nothing ever happened before."

"Don't worry. It did its job. That's what it's there for. Come in tomorrow, and we'll check it out."

And that was the beginning of our slippery slope.

Over the next eight months, Joe would frequently be hospitalized—sometimes for four days, and other times two weeks. Nothing ever went smoothly. On one occasion, on being released from the hospital after a two-week stay, we were on our way home when I glanced over at Joe and saw that he was pale. He instructed me to pull over to the shoulder of the parkway. Within seconds after stopping the car, the defibrillator fired. I raced back to the hospital, left Joe in the ER parking lot, and ran past the desk directly back up to the unit Joe had just been discharged from. I spied the nurse who had been Joe's primary caregiver over the past two weeks.

"Tim, Tim!" I screamed.

Tim turned around and looked at me quizzically. "Tim, the defibrillator fired on our way home," I told him.

"Where is he?" Tim asked hurriedly.

"In the ER parking lot, in the car."

"I'm taking the stairs," Tim yelled over his shoulder as he sprinted down the hall. I followed right behind him. He ran past the ER desk, grabbing a wheelchair on his way out the double doors to the parking lot. After helping Joe out of the car and into the chair, he flew by the desk one more time and went directly to the cardiac unit located in the ER. I found out later that this is called the FAST TRACK, set up specifically for emergency cases of cardiac arrest. Joe was hooked up to monitors, and Dr. Germano was paged. Unfortunately, he had already left the hospital, but Tim was determined to track him down, and he finally did. With Dr. Germano on the phone, the ER staff and Tim explained what had happened and read the output from all the machines. By this time, Joe was feeling better—shaken up but okay. Dr. Germano asked, "Joe, are you okay? What happened? What did you feel?"

"I felt fine, but then I knew it was going to fire. I now can tell, I can feel it coming on. I told Jane to pull over. I didn't want it to happen while she was driving. But I feel okay now. I just can't believe it happened. Two weeks in the hospital and now this?"

"I can't believe it either, Joe. We monitored you for two weeks; everything was fine. We adjusted the defibrillator, we adjusted your medication. Go home and get some rest. I'll see you next week in my office."

That's how it went for the next eight months. At one point, a more advanced defibrillator was put in. Then an ablation was recommended. We had never heard this term before, and when it was explained to us it didn't reassure us. Cardiac ablation is a procedure that can correct arrhythmias. It works by scarring or destroying tissue in your heart that triggers or sustains an abnormal heart rhythm. Dr. Germano was wonderful about explaining it to us in the simplest terms possible, but we were still apprehensive.

After the ablation, Dr. Germano decided to keep Joe overnight to monitor him. He wasn't the average patient. At about 10 p.m. I received a call.

"Hi, Mrs. Bavoso. Joe Germano here. I don't want to upset you, but Joe was put on a ventilator tonight. He was having trouble breathing, and we decided he needed some help after the procedure. It's only temporary. He should be off of it by morning. I'm positive he'll be discharged tomorrow. I know this is a shock, but he's going to be okay. I'll see you in the morning."

The next morning, Joe was off the ventilator, and he did come home, but he was very distressed. The experience of being on the ventilator really shook him up, which was clear as he shared his story with me.

"I woke up around midnight," he said. "I know it was midnight because there was a wall clock in front of me. I could see the nurse at her station, and then I realized I couldn't speak, that I was on a ventilator. No one came into the room, and I couldn't call out. I was confused and scared to death. And then I looked up and I saw my brother Danny standing there, and he looked at me, smiled, and waved."

I was speechless. Danny, Joe's younger brother, had passed away two years earlier while preparing for a bone marrow transplant. Joe was a match and was planning on being the donor. However, Danny died of complications from an infection before the transplant could take place. It was a terrible blow to Joe. I wasn't sure what to say.

"Joe, you were under sedation. He was probably on your mind."

"I saw him, Jane. He was there."

"Well then, take comfort in that. He was telling you everything would be okay."

Joe never mentioned that incident again. It tortured him, as did the thought of again being put on a ventilator.

When we saw Dr. Germano the following week, he discussed with us a drug called Amiodarone, which is used to treat ventricular fibrillation and ventricular tachycardia.

"This drug works, Joe, but the side effects are pretty grim. It usually takes about ten years for the side effects to become a major problem, but you're too young for that right now. You'd only be in your early seventies, and we'd like to see you live a long life," explained Dr. Germano, "so I'm not comfortable using it."

But then, during one of Joe's frequent hospital stays, Amiodarone was administered to Joe through an IV. The situation was becoming more grave. Because of the use of the drug, we were now introduced to a kidney and pulmonary doctor. Joe's creatinine level was higher than normal, so he was monitored for kidney function. The young nephrologist was friendly and kind, and after a few visits, he and Joe bonded, which was becoming the norm with Joe and most of the doctors he met along the way. By this time, I was accompanying Joe to most of his doctor appointments. The nephrologist looked at him and said, "Joe, I want you to live well into your eighties. You're a perfect candidate for a heart transplant. When the time comes, you're going to do great."

I never said a word to Joe about that comment; it was too ominous for me. I knew in my heart that a transplant was going to happen, but I wanted to believe it was years away. I was definitely in denial. I couldn't even think about such an undertaking.

But Thanksgiving Day brought a reality check.

Joe was hospitalized again in the beginning of November 2008. It was another long stretch—two weeks. I went to the hospital every night after work and stayed until visiting hours were over. As I was getting ready to leave one evening, I kissed Joe goodbye and told him I would call him when I got home. He held my hand, looked me in the eyes, and told me, "I hate the thought of you walking into an empty house all alone."

"I'll be fine, and besides, you'll be home in a few days," I reassured him.

Those words haunted me in the months that followed. Joe was released from the hospital in time for Thanksgiving. Lauren was hosting dinner. Since Joe and I got married, we always spent Thanksgiving with his family, and this year was no exception. There would be more than thirty of us, including Joe's parents. The day was wonderful and Joe was feeling especially thankful. After grace, he stood up and raised his glass.

"I just want to thank everyone for the support you've given me and Jane during this past year. I don't think I would have gotten through it without your love and prayers. I feel so blessed to be here with my whole family tonight. Thank you, guys. I love you all."

It was a special moment that brought tears to everyone's eyes. When dinner was over, everyone was milling around chatting and laughing and helping with the cleanup. I was in the kitchen with Joe standing next to me, holding court as usual, when all of a sudden he let out the most god-awful sound. I jumped and looked over at him—the defibrillator had fired! Joe was still standing, but was pale. My sister-in-law got him to a chair and started taking his pulse. Joe was okay, but of course he was shaken up. Once again, two weeks in the hospital, everything perfect, and then this. I took him home and called the hospital to speak to one of the cardiologists. I was instructed to bring him in. By midnight I was driving to Winthrop Hospital.

After spending another few days there, he was released. We managed to celebrate Christmas with our children and grandchildren but we cancelled our annual Christmas party that we hosted every year for fifty people. Joe was still too weak from his last incident.

We quietly welcomed in 2009 and after the New Year, we saw Drs. Marzo and Germano again. We all agreed to make an appointment to see Dr. Donna Mancini, the head of the heart transplant team, at Columbia Presbyterian Hospital in Manhattan.

CHAPTER NINE

Getting There

G etting an appointment at Columbia proved to be no easy task. I was
accustomed to Joe always managing things, and I knew this time
wouldn't be any different. Joe was always the rock, the strong one, the person
everyone depended on. I couldn't imagine it any other way. The thought of
him actually undergoing a heart transplant was surreal. We never seemed
to discuss it much; we knew it was going to happen at some point but we—
mostly me—wanted things to be ordinary, even though normalcy had managed to evade us for quite a while. So I sat back and let Joe take charge, as
he had done for most of his life.

As the oldest of six children, Joe was often left in charge when his parents were out for the evening. The firstborn, according to his siblings, could
do no wrong in their mother's eyes. I never sensed any resentment among
the other five toward Joe; they accepted that he took the place of his parents
when their mom and dad weren't around. Well, maybe all of them except
Danny. Danny was always the feisty one, the rulebreaker. I can remember
walking into the house one Saturday night and hearing screams from the
front bedroom. I looked at the other four, who were calmly watching TV,
and asked, "What's going on?"

"Oh, Danny's giving Joe a hard time," they answered off-handedly as
they continued to watch their favorite TV show.

The screams were growing louder as I quickly walked into the bedroom and saw Joe with Danny pinned under him, fists flying. I yelled, "Joe, stop it, stop it right now. You're going to kill him," which, of course, was the hysteria of a fifteen-year-old girl. I was the youngest of six, and although my brother and I often argued, it never came to blows, so this was quite a shock for me. They then got up off the floor and walked away from each other; it was as simple as that. But Joe had established that he was in charge.

When Joe was ready for high school, he rejected his mother's plan to send him to an all-boys Catholic school. "No way am I going to be beaten up four more years by nuns. I'm going to the public high school," he emphatically told his mom. The public school he would attend was considered pretty rough, so his mother begged and pleaded with him to go to the nice, safe Catholic school, but Joe held his ground. When I met him in his sophomore year, he explained to me how he managed to have no problems in school. "I just got to know all the gang leaders and made friends with them," he told me one night. "They don't bother me, and I don't bother them." Again, it was as simple as that.

After being dropped from the football team, Joe joined the band and learned how to play the drums. That was the start of his career as a drummer, which followed him throughout his life. For the next several decades, Joe played in a variety of bands at different venues, including the 1964 World's Fair. In the beginning, it put money in his pocket to take me to the movies and for a slice of pizza on a Saturday night, and then eventually it put money in the bank to help us save for a house.

Being from a large family, Joe was taught that if you wanted something, you had to earn it yourself; there were no handouts. I never remember Joe without a job. From the age of ten or eleven, when he had a paper route, until the day he died, Joe had a job. He worked in delis and coffee shops, in the caverns of the main library at Grand Army Plaza in Brooklyn, and even as a camp counselor during a few summers. And, of course, he was always in a band.

When he became a dad, there was never a question about who would fix the broken bike chain, oil the baseball glove, untangle the fishing line, mold the mouthpiece, buy the cleats, or go to the batting range. If any kid needed a ride to practice or to a game, they knew they could call Mr. B. because Mr. B. was always there and willing to pick them up. When Joe noticed that Lauren was being put in goal at some of her soccer games, he immediately bought her a mouth guard. This piece of equipment was not a requirement at the time, and Lauren balked at the idea of wearing one. "No one else wears one, dad," she lamented.

"I really don't care," replied Joe. "I'm not going to watch my daughter's teeth get kicked out of her mouth. If the coach puts you in goal, I better see you put that mouthpiece in." And the mouthpiece always went in.

It was the same when Peter played football. The equipment provided by the league was top-notch at the time, but it didn't include a neck brace. So Joe got a neck brace for his son.

When he coached Little League, his one rule was that every boy on his team was required to wear an athletic cup. That sounds rather basic today, but in the early eighties it was not a requirement. Before every practice and game, Joe would line up his team of nine-year-olds, walk down the line and, with his knuckle, gently tap each boy to confirm whether he was wearing a cup. If a boy wasn't wearing the equipment, he was benched with an explanation of why it was important to comply with the coach's rule. He instructed his players, "Go home and tell your parents on this team you need a cup."

When a parent would complain about their son being benched, Joe's answer was always the same. "On my team you wear a cup. I don't want to see any kid get hurt. Besides, don't you want grandchildren someday?" That remark was usually met with a chuckle, and the next time the kid showed up, he would be wearing a cup.

Yeah, Joe was in charge.

So I stepped aside and let Joe take control of making an appointment at Columbia. It turned out to be more difficult than expected because of miscommunications or a paperwork mix-up at the hospital, and it was beginning to frustrate both of us. In the meantime, Joe's parents, both elderly, were experiencing health problems. We were driving back and forth to Brooklyn to see his mother, who at this point needed an aide and was getting near the end of her life. Joe, the usual driver in the family, sat in the passenger seat while I navigated the Belt Parkway, as Joe was too physically and emotionally drained to combat the traffic. He was facing his mother's imminent death and his own health crisis. In the midst of all this, his ninety-two-year-old father required a pacemaker.

I saw a definite change in him in March. His pallor was turning gray, and he had lost weight. We had an appointment with Drs. Marzo and Germano on March 31, 2009. Joe was ready with a list of concerns he had typed up to discuss with the doctors:

In the past eight months, I've spent 31 days in the hospital.

My plans for retirement were put off due to the economy and replaced with semi-retirement.

The extra time during semi-retirement was to continue the development of my photography business. I have not shot a photograph since June 2008.

I may have to cancel four art shows that I was invited to.

My driving is restricted to short trips, but it has been suggested that I stop driving altogether. If I stop driving, I have no way to get to work, even on a semi-retired basis.

I've given up golf.

I've given up my boat.

I've been unsuccessful in getting an initial consultation with Dr. Mancini to discuss a possible transplant.

Two weeks ago, both my parents fell ill.

The following day, my dad, 92, had a pacemaker implanted. The following Monday, my mom, 89, died, and we buried her on March 27.

I feel tired and fatigued, partly due to allergies causing post-nasal drip and an almost constant cough keeping me awake most nights, interrupting eating and normal conversation. My CHF is probably contributing to this situation as well, but I believe most is caused by anxiety and depression.

That was the first time I heard Joe use the word depression. No matter what happened to him, no matter how many times he was in the hospital, he always remained upbeat. The person who was always in charge was now losing control, and the only way he knew how to handle it was to write it all down.

Finally, as always, Joe prevailed. He managed to get an appointment with Dr. Donna Mancini, for the day after Mother's Day, May 2009. Just for a moment, Joe felt in control once more.

CHAPTER TEN

FINALLY

Mother's Day of 2009 found us spending a few hours at Lauren's house before we set off for the city. Joe suggested that we stay Sunday night at a hotel near the hospital.

"You know I don't think I could get up that early to make it into the city for a 9:30 a.m. appointment," he said. "I get tired too easily now."

I was a little surprised; this wasn't like him. Although he had given up most of his hobbies, he was still going to work three days a week and puttering around the house, taking care of things. He found a little hotel that was reasonable and made a reservation for two nights. We had been advised that the consultation plus testing would take two full days.

I watched as he played with the children. Hannah, the baby, was only eight months old, the twins were twenty-two months, and the oldest was four. They giggled as he interacted with them, and I knew how much he wanted to roll on the floor with them or throw them in the air, but he satisfied himself with less physical play.

We took the train to the city in the late afternoon and caught a cab to the hotel. It was a cozy little place, and at one time it may have been a small apartment house. The lobby didn't consist of much besides the check-in desk and maybe a chair or two. The elevator was tiny and to the right of the desk. When we got to our floor, we decided it must have been an apartment building at one time, the open stairway being directly across from the elevator. There were only a few rooms on the floor, and we found ours easily. It was small, but clean and functional. "Well, it's not the Waldorf, but it'll do," quipped Joe.

"I like it," I answered. "It's cute."

At another time, it would have been a fun experience for us. We loved going into the city, and finding a little hotel off the beaten path would have been an adventure. We would have visited a museum, had a nice dinner, and come home the next day to tell our kids all about it. But unfortunately it wasn't another time—it was this time.

We found a diner next door to the hotel and had something to eat, even though neither of us was particularly hungry. Reality was setting in. We were really here, getting ready for our appointment at Columbia to discuss a transplant. We went back up to the room and tried to get some sleep, but sleep eluded both of us.

In the morning, we walked across the street to a Starbucks for some tea and coffee and then hailed a cab to take us to the hospital. We had asked Peter and Lauren to attend the consultation with us, wanting them involved in this major decision. We were happy to see them when they both pulled up in cabs.

We found the correct office and, after giving our name, were directed to a large conference room. Sitting around the table were members of the transplant team. Doctors, nurses, a social worker, a psychiatrist, and finance people made up the group. The four of us were seated, and the interrogation began. We were asked about our background, our family, friends, social groups we belonged to, churches we attended. The surgery was explained to us, how the match would be made, how long it usually takes to get a heart, the aftercare, the drugs that were involved, the rehab. "It's very important," we were told, "that you have support from family and friends." We were warned that besides the physical challenges of a transplant, there are also psychological challenges.

I glanced sideways at Joe and watched as he sat up straighter in his chair. He leaned forward a bit and placed his crossed arms on the table. He looked around at each of his inquisitors, making sure he caught their eyes, and then he said, "Jane and I have been together since high school. We'll be married forty-one years in September. We're rock-solid. My two children are here with us today. We consider their spouses our own children. My wife and I are both from large families. I'm the oldest of six, and Jane is the youngest of six. I have numerous friends from all walks of my life. The one thing you don't have to worry about is support. My goal is to get my life back. Jane's goal is to get our life back. I have plans for the future. All I ask is that you give me a shot and put me on the list."

At that moment, Joe and I would never have guessed how much support we would receive from what we eventually started calling "our village."

Then Joe coughed a little and excused himself, explaining, "Sorry, I have allergies."

The nurse sitting at the table looked across at Joe and said knowingly, "You might have allergies, but that's a congestive heart failure cough."

I shouldn't have been, but I was startled by that comment. After all, Joe was here to be evaluated for a heart transplant. But he had been coughing for months, had seen an allergist, and was prescribed allergy medication. We didn't—or maybe I didn't—connect the two. I wanted to believe that a transplant wouldn't be needed immediately. I was always trying to fool myself.

After the consultation we were sent to the finance department. We were again interrogated, but this time about our insurance. Coverage, co-pays, cost of hospital stays, and so on bounced around the room. We were fortunate that we had excellent coverage. That made the finance person smile. She was probably silently giving thanks that this appointment would be an easy one.

Finally, we met with the head of the transplant team, Dr. Donna Mancini. She wasn't at all what we expected. A very petite woman, she was kind but not warm and fuzzy. After examining Joe, she remarked, "I'm glad Dr. Marzo got you up here to see me."

We were glad too, but her demeanor and the way she uttered that statement sent shivers up my spine. "Let's get some testing done, and then we can evaluate you better."

We were then shuffled into a waiting room to be called in to begin the testing. As I looked around the crowded room, I saw people of all ages and ethnic backgrounds. Most were there for checkups after their transplants. Some of them joked with each other asking, "What room were you in? Did you have a view?" Most had received kidney transplants; one had had a heart transplant eleven years earlier. I looked at these people, and instead of feeling hopeful, terror struck me. I didn't want Joe to be in their club.

Finally, Joe's name was called by a friendly and cheerful nurse. She introduced herself as Maggie and told us she had been a nurse at Columbia dealing with transplant patients for over twenty years. She then waved to the young man who had the heart transplant. "Hi, Ed. How many years has it been?"

"Eleven," answered Ed.

Looking at us, she smiled her big, happy smile. "Look how great he's doing! We perform miracles here!"

I prayed she was right.

Maggie took Joe with her and told the three of us that he would be back soon, and after some initial testing we could all leave. Considering the circumstances, Maggie was the most cheerful person I ever met. An hour later, Maggie wasn't so cheerful anymore. "We have a problem," she told us. "The pressure in the heart is so low we can't release him. I can't believe this man has been working! That's incredible. I'm trying to get him a bed; he has to stay the night."

What the hell happened? I thought. An hour ago we were here for a consultation, and now he has to be admitted? My head was spinning, and I couldn't think straight.

"You can come see him. He's in a bed waiting for a room." Obediently, we all followed Maggie in a line. As I watched Joe lying in the bed, I thought, *He's so calm. Why is he so calm?* Now, as I think back, maybe he was just so tired of trying to keep everything together, and he realized he didn't have to anymore. This happy, smiley nurse was going to take care of him.

I heard Maggie on the phone talking to the admitting department. "Come on, you have to find a bed for this nice man. Seriously, this guy is one of the nicest people I've met—find him a room."

I smiled to myself when I heard her cajoling the person on the phone. Obviously, Joe had won her over in just a short while.

The testing began, and it revealed that Joe was retaining water, although it wasn't showing in his ankles. We were both so diligent regarding his fluid levels. Joe weighed himself every morning. Any weight gain of two pounds or more was addressed by adjusting his diuretics. I cooked without salt, and Joe read every label and was extremely conscientious about anything he ate outside of our home. We checked his ankles every day. So when we were told that he was retaining water, it came as the second shock of the day.

He was put on IV diuretics and a drug that would help the pumping of his heart. The doctors decided that a peripherally inserted central catheter, also known as a picc line, would be inserted in a vein. He would wear a fanny pack to come home so the medicine would be automatically pumped into his system. We also learned the structure of the transplant list: 1A: people in the hospital; 1B: people at home with a picc line or other apparatus; 2: people at home just on medication. The plan at the moment was to evaluate Joe and make a decision by Friday regarding his status. All the tests that were going to be done as an outpatient would now be done in the hospital. The staff was excited that Joe had type A blood. They assured us it was much easier to get a heart with type A blood than with type O.

I couldn't keep track of what they were telling me. "No, no!" I wanted to shout at them. "You're talking about the wrong person. We're just here for a consultation. Joe went to work last week. You've got the wrong patient."

A room was finally found in the cardiac care unit. I guess it was the best they had on such short notice because it was cold and depressing, located in a dark corner of the floor with the AC dripping overhead. The thought of leaving Joe there horrified me. The three of us were dumbfounded, speechless, me even more so than my children.

"Mom, Mom," they called to me.

"What?" I answered in a fog.

"Mom, what do you want to do? Do you want to go back to the hotel? It'd be closer for you to get back to the hospital tomorrow."

I woke up from my fog. "I think I want to go home."

"Are you sure? It would be so much easier for you to just stay in the city."

"No, I need to be home."

"Okay, Mom, whatever you want."

And so I went home and waited for the next day to come with Dr. Mancini's words resonating in my head—"Glad Dr. Marzo got you up here to see me."

CHAPTER ELEVEN

THE CLIMB GETS STEEPER

The picc line was put in on the following Monday, May 18. We were told that the line would have to be checked every other day for four days, so Joe would remain in the hospital until the following week. He was also scheduled for a kidney biopsy the next day.

On May 20, the biopsy came back normal; the protein they were looking for wasn't there. That was a good sign, but renal failure was feared because the heart wasn't pumping properly, so another catheter was inserted into Joe's neck to once again check the pressure of his heart. The doctors discussed putting a balloon pump around Joe's aorta to help with the blood flow to the kidneys.

That night, Marty arrived at the hospital after work. As the hours passed, he finally called Lauren. "Listen, your dad's having a rough time right now, and I don't want to leave him. Don't expect me home until late." He never left Joe's side until 11:00 p.m., although the next day he would have to be in the city early for work.

At 6:00 a.m. the next morning, I called the nurse on duty after a sleepless night.

"Just a minute, Mrs. Bavoso, let me check his chart."

I paced, as I always do when I'm nervous. It seemed like forever before she got back to me. "Well, for now," she said, "the medicine seems to be working, so the pump isn't scheduled at this time. Some fluid has accumulated in his lungs and he's being treated with Lasix." Lasix is a diuretic used to treat fluid retention caused by congestive heart failure.

On my way to the hospital later, I kept asking myself, *How did this all go bad so quickly?* I was thinking about Joe going to work the week before. I couldn't get that out of my mind, that this man got into his car and drove to work. Considering the circumstances we were now in, I questioned how he could have possibly done that. How bad must he have felt? How had he managed to push himself to hold down a job? But then again, Joe never took time off from work. I remembered years before, when we were so much younger, he had developed bronchitis. Orders from the doctor were, "Joe, this could lead to pneumonia. I want you to take a few days off." And the next day I just shook my head as I watched him drive to the office.

Everything changed from hour to hour. What we were told at 10:00 a.m. would change by noon. May 21 was filled with consultations. We spoke with the transplant doctor, the cardiologist, the nurse practitioner, and the kidney doctor, who was now also included in the mix.

Information was thrown at us from every direction. Joe was getting weaker, and he looked awful. His color was gray, and he was lethargic. It was the first time I thought I might lose him, and the fear tightened my chest as I sat by his bedside. By evening, the decision was made to put in the balloon pump to try and help with the water retention. We were informed that the pump could be kept in for up to ten days. They were planning to implant a left ventricular assist device, also known as an LVAD, which is referred to as a bridge to transplant. This would enable Joe to stay alive until a heart became available, but before they could implant the LVAD they had to get rid of the water.

As I was leaving the hospital that night, Joe looked at me, exhausted, and the weakest I had ever seen him. He held my hand and quietly said, "I guess I won't be able to see my babies for a long time."

My heart broke in two. Joe was the doting grandfather. He was at the hospital with his camera shooting pictures from the moment we were allowed to peek at our new grandchildren. His babies, as he always referred to them, ran to him whenever they saw us. I don't know if I was feeling anger or sadness, or maybe it was a combination, but all I could think was how cruel and unfair this was.

I managed to take a deep breath and looked him in the eye while assuring him that when he did see them, he would be stronger, and he could finally play with them like he longed to do. I had begun to realize that it was going to be my job to keep hope alive.

Finally, I heard the words we were waiting to hear: "Mrs. Bavoso, your husband will be presented Friday morning as a candidate for transplant." We all held our breath until Friday, praying that he would immediately be put on the transplant list.

Friends were starting to reach out to us. One had a connection with Columbia and inquired as to the name of Joe's doctor and what room he was in. If there is one thing I've learned over the years, it's good to have friends with connections who are willing to use them to help you out. Our village was beginning to grow.

On May 23, Joe was officially put on the transplant list as a priority. The LVAD was scheduled to be implanted on Monday, May 25. Joe had now been in the hospital for fifteen days. Although the pump was getting some of the water out, Joe was weakening rapidly, and the team decided he needed the LVAD ASAP. It was a three-hour operation followed by a four-week hospital stay. I was told I would be instructed on how to care for and maintain the device.

He received the LVAD as scheduled. The surgery was done by Dr. Naka, who at the time was the only doctor who implanted LVADs at Columbia. He was considered the best of the best, but we already knew that. Peter had been Googling every doctor at Columbia who had anything to do with heart transplants. We were well aware of Dr. Naka's background and his credentials before we even met him. After the surgery Dr. Naka advised us, "There were some minor repairs that needed to be done, but I want you to know that they didn't contribute in any way to your husband's heart failure. He's now temporarily on a ventilator. He's heavily sedated and on strong pain medication. Everything went well. This will enable him to get stronger for the transplant."

The next day, the breathing tube was removed but had to be reinserted because Joe had developed pneumonia and was being treated with three different antibiotics. Dr. Naka apprised us of the situation. "Pneumonia," he said, "is very typical after being in the hospital for two weeks and then undergoing major surgery. Your husband has no fever, and his cultures are coming back negative. He should be fine in a few days." And so I did what I would be finding myself doing over many months: I put my trust in the experts.

When I finally got to see Joe, even though he was still on the ventilator, his color looked good—so much better than the day before—and he was writing me messages. Funny messages. He hadn't lost his sense of humor; he was feeling better and positive. After all, this was Columbia, and as Maggie the nurse had told us, "We perform miracles here."

On May 30, the breathing tube was removed, and Joe was sitting up in a chair, the first time he had been out of bed in three weeks. I was told he was doing well, and his color looked better than it had in six months. The LVAD was doing its job. He still had a feeding tube and some IVs, but I felt we were on our way. We still had so far to go, but we were definitely on our way.

CHAPTER TWELVE

ONWARD

On June 3, Joe was put in a step-down unit, and that's when our relationship with Dave the physical therapist began. This smiling, confident, happy young man walked into the room and introduced himself.

"Hi, Mr. Bavoso, I'm Dave Zemmel and I'm going to be your physical therapist."

"Good to meet you Dave." You couldn't help but immediately connect with Dave. His smile was infectious, his personality warm and caring.

"Mind if I call you Joe?" Dave asked. "We'll be working closely together for the next few weeks to get you in shape for the transplant".

"No problem with that, Dave. Just get me where I need to be."

"Ok, then," Dave sprang into action, "Let's get you up and on your feet. We have to get you strong again, and I promise if you follow my instructions, you'll be ready for that new heart."

Dave was pretty impressed with the first session, and he commented on how well Joe did.

"Great start, Joe. I know you feel wobbly, but I promise you that with each session you'll begin to feel stronger and more confident."

At the side of the bed was a machine called a Power Backup Unit (PBU) that Joe was attached to. All the wires from the small system controller he had strapped around his waist were connected to this device, keeping the LVAD pumping. When Joe was detached from the machine, two large batteries worn in a harness strapped over his shoulders would be attached to the device, making Joe more mobile. Extra batteries were always charging in the PBU. All of this was not only alien but downright scary. This machine was keeping Joe alive, and I had to learn all of its workings and be ready to correct any glitches that might happen when Joe came home. Right now I was just getting used to looking at it, and it was intimidating.

The real instructions would begin when Joe was discharged from the step-down unit. Dave gave us a quick overview of how the LVAD worked, but I didn't absorb too much of it at the time. It was overwhelming, and the thought of all this responsibility resting on my shoulders frightened me. I stood there thinking, *How am I going to do this? I don't want to do this—I want someone else to be in charge. What if I screw up, make a mistake, forget what the signals mean?*

I could feel the panic swell. I kept saying to myself, *I'm not a medical person. I don't want Joe's life in my hands.* I would have gladly handed this role over to anyone who would take it, but there wasn't anyone else. There was just me, and I was terrified. I silently prayed for courage.

On June 4 I saw two other men walking in the hall with an LVAD. Strangely, it was comforting to me knowing that we weren't alone. There were other people hoping, struggling, and praying just like us. Maybe it's the old adage "Misery loves company," but for some reason it made me feel better. I walked into Joe's room and kiddingly said, "Hey, guess what? You're in an exclusive club. I just saw some of your members walking down the hall." He gave me that look that told me he didn't think I was very funny.

We were then visited by an administrator of patient services. Virginia had been sent to us by our friend who had some pull at Columbia. She inquired whether we needed anything or if she could help us in any way.

"No," we answered together. "Everything's fine, and so far all the people we've met have been helpful."

"Well, that's good to hear. But here's my card with my direct number just in case anything comes up that you need to speak with me about."

That evening Joe walked further than he had the day before, and the LVAD nurse was very pleased. They upped his diuretics because he was still retaining water in his ankles. Friday night he was transferred from the step-down unit to a private room with the most fantastic view of the Hudson River. Virginia had come through.

Joe was now in the hands of the LVAD nurses, a team of five women. Margaret was the nurse in charge. She was a no-nonsense, follow-the-rules type of manager. She knew her job well and expected her nurses to know theirs. She was a wealth of information and had the answer to any question we asked. She constantly urged Joe to walk as much as he could to get in shape for the transplant. She and Joe shared a love of photography, and she would often ask Joe's opinion about a camera or lens. They had found a common ground besides an LVAD.

Khristine, a beautiful young woman, was new to the team. She seemed to be intimidated in the beginning by Margaret's iron hand and came across as abrasive when we first met her. After a couple of weeks, she melted our heart. She was warm and kind, and when she got to know us, she knew she could let her guard down.

Rosie was a senior member on the team but didn't have much inter-action with Joe. Donna was the administrative assistant, keeping track of the mountains of paperwork attached to each patient.

And then there was Jennifer, known to everyone as Jenn. Joe spoke of her all the time, but it took me a while to meet her; she always seemed to have finished her rounds by the time I got to the hospital. She was Joe's favorite. When I finally did meet her, I knew why. Jenn had a wide smile; she was funny and quirky and teased Joe about everything. It turned out she was a Civil War buff like Joe, and they shared many stories of the war and books they had read. Jenn eventually became our angel in more ways than one.

The sixth week seemed to be Joe's turnaround. He finally started feeling and sounding more like himself. On June 21, his last IV was removed, and although he was still on oxygen, his levels seemed to be stable. Dave had Joe walking once a day, a little farther each time. He was still weak, and the doctors were trying to build him up with supplements. They decided to upgrade his meal plan as another way to help him get stronger. The next day, June 22, marked seven weeks that Joe had been in the hospital.

At the time, Ed Koch, the onetime mayor of New York, was also at the hospital on the same floor as Joe for a bypass and valve replacement. Joe and I joked that he was now hanging with the big guns, and he was probably eating the same upgraded dinner as the former mayor. Anything that could make us smile, even for a moment, was a welcome relief because there was no talk yet of sending Joe home.

By this time, we had a large following of what we started to refer to as "Joe's Journey." I shared with Joe the emails people sent, inquiring about his progress, and I brought him all of the many get well and prayer cards that filled my mailbox each day. I wanted him to know that he wasn't forgotten, that people were praying and pulling for him. After reading all of the cards and notes, he looked at me with a little smirk on his face and said, "Well, I guess I didn't piss off too many people in my life." And that's when I knew Joe was on his way back.

On July 1, week eight in the hospital, Dave gave Joe permission to take a walk down the hall with a family member. Joe and I took a stroll all by ourselves. No nurses hovering by, no one giving Joe instructions, just the two of us, almost carefree, pretending we were strolling along the water's edge in Montauk, Joe snapping pictures of the waves crashing to shore and me carrying his equipment. Just like when times were good.

Joe did well, stopping only once because his legs weakened. I couldn't have imagined Joe's legs ever being weak. He looked great in a pair of shorts, and I always told him I thought he had the best guy legs I ever saw. They were strong and muscular, and even as he aged, they stayed that way. He always laughed and said it was probably from all the years of delivering the paper in Brooklyn.

The doctors were hoping to release Joe within ten to fourteen days.

"We won't hold them to that," was Joe's reply. He didn't want to be disappointed if it didn't happen.

CHAPTER THIRTEEN

Trying for Some Normalcy

During the weeks Joe was in the hospital, normal wasn't in our vocabulary. Each day brought a new challenge, and all I wanted was for my life to once again become predictable and mundane. I longed for the days of so-called boredom when every day seemed like the last and a small diversion from the humdrum of life's daily grind was much sought after.

While Joe was struggling to gain back his strength, preparations had to be made for his return home. An electrical outlet devoted solely to the PBU was required to be installed in our bedroom. Grab bars in the shower were needed. The local fire department and electric company had to be informed of Joe's status; he would be put on a priority list in case of any electrical outages.

My job was to learn the workings of the system controller, which was attached to the LVAD to keep the device pumping. The pump diverts blood from the weakened left side of the heart and propels it onward. The system controller, with its internal computer program, regulates the pump. The PBU powered the LVAD while Joe was tethered to it during the night. It also charged and tested the batteries. The PBU cable connected the PBU to the system controller. There were two color-coded connectors—black and white. There was a display module that, when connected to the PBU, provided a display of system performance. We were also given an EEP, or emergency power pack. This would provide up to twelve hours of power in the event of an outage. The system controller keypad was composed of two buttons, a battery, fuel gauges, and four alarm symbols.

I was given a booklet to study that explained what every signal and color meant on the system controller. I was also given a CD to learn how to change out the system controller for a new one in case of a glitch. We were required to always have a backup controller. If there was a glitch and the controller needed to be switched, it had to be done in a matter of minutes because, for Joe, it meant life or death. So, on my train rides to and from the hospital, I studied the booklet from cover to cover. On my arrival home each evening I popped in the CD until I had every step memorized.

The next thing I was trained to do was to change the dressing that covered the driveline, which extended from the internal pump out of the skin to the system controller. This had to be done under completely sterile conditions. The dressing had to be changed every other day. The nurse who performed this procedure in the hospital had me watch her several times before I would be tested. Rubber gloves were donned, and both the patient and person performing the dressing change were required to wear a mask. A sterile towel was removed from its wrapping, and I was instructed to grab it at the very edge and pull it out with my fingertips. It was then placed on a small table to hold the other apparatus needed for the change. The old bandage was then removed. The rubber gloves were exchanged for sterile ones. The next step was to put on the sterile gloves without touching the outside; the first glove is easy to get on, but the second one is trickier. It took me a few tries to master the technique. When I would get frustrated with myself, the nurse was encouraging. "You're doing great," she would tell me. "Some people never get it right. And remember, I learned this in nursing school. So don't beat yourself up."

The next step is to clean the area around the cable, swabbing in circles, continually working outward. Then the new bandages were applied. There would be two over the opening and another to adhere the cable tightly so it wouldn't be jarred.

This whole procedure freaked me out. I knew that any mistakes could cause infection, which is the most frightening word in a hospital, especially with an LVAD or heart transplant patient. My heart pounded in my chest each time I was required to observe because I knew Joe wouldn't be released until I passed both a written test on the workings of the system controller and a hands-on test of the dressing change.

While all this was going on, I was still trying to hold down my job that I'd had for the last twenty years. I was employed at a privately owned manufacturing company with an office staff of six women. We all got along well, and when Joe's heart issues became more serious, I received an incredible amount of support from both my fellow coworkers and management. I had to be at the hospital at least two days a week, and many times over the whole nine weeks I was there for three or more, especially in the beginning when things were touch and go. I was thankful I never felt any pressure of losing my job or sensed any resentment from my coworkers when they had to pick up the slack that was caused by my absence.

I needed this job to hold on to my sanity. I needed to know that for a couple of days a week, everything was almost normal. Getting up when the alarm rang, walking on my treadmill, gulping down some breakfast, driving to the office, greeting my fellow coworkers, and settling at my desk for the day gave me some sense of comfort. I was trying to deal with chaos and uncertainty in my life, so these few days a week helped me push into a little corner of my mind the mayhem that had taken over.

Changes were also happening at the company, and a new CFO was hired. I would now be answering directly to him. He called me and my two coworkers, who worked in the accounting department, separately into the conference room to introduce himself and discuss his goals and how we would accomplish them. I was nervous. I had no relationship with this man, and he had no loyalty to me. I wasn't even sure if he knew of my circumstances, but I did know that my fate was now in his hands.

I entered the room hesitantly and was greeted with a handshake and smile. "Well, Jane, I've only heard good things about you, and after reviewing your past performance I know we'll work well together."

"Thank you. I appreciate that." And then we went over the normal topics that come up - procedures, reports, timelines, and so on.

"So, Jane, do you have any questions for me?"

And that's when my heart started to race. I had to be honest with this man, and I was hoping it wouldn't jeopardize this job that I now needed more than ever. So I took a deep breath and started. "Well, I'm not sure if you're aware of my circumstances, but my husband is waiting to be put on the transplant list to receive a new heart. When that happens, I'm going to need some extended time off to help him get back on his feet. I just want to be upfront with you."

He looked at me kindly and said, "I'm fully aware of what's going on in your life right now. Don't worry about it. We'll deal with it when the time comes." I breathed a big sigh of relief. It felt like a ten-ton weight had been lifted off my shoulders. Maybe for a little while, I thought, I would be able to keep some small fraction of normalcy in my life.

CHAPTER FOURTEEN

At Last

After so many weeks, we were all getting antsy as the day of Joe's discharge came closer. While I was working on feeling more confident with the dressing change and learning the workings of the system controller, Joe was working on getting stronger. Soon, the time arrived for us both to be tested. We were put in a small room where we were both handed a questionnaire. I commented, "Well, they either trust us not to cheat, or they expect us to help each other." We both aced the test.

I was then measured on the dressing change. The nurse stood by my side and observed as I took charge of the procedure while Joe lay calmly watching. The thought occurred to me whether he'd be this confident when we were home and I'd be performing this task unsupervised. I passed the inspection without a hitch.

We were going home!

After lots of instructions and goodbyes, we walked into our house on Monday, July 13, nine weeks after Joe was first admitted. He came home with oxygen, having been assured it was temporary. Joe was using a spirometer or Air Life apparatus, which helps the lungs recover after surgery. He inquired about using weights to help build up his muscle mass. Joe was determined to do everything he could to prepare for the transplant.

The next day we were visited by a home care nurse, Marie. After her evaluation, she was sure that Joe wouldn't need her for long. He was setting goals for himself. On Wednesday, July 15, he wrote in the journal he had been keeping since all this began:

I'm still hitting 1250 on Air Life and should get to this week's goal of 1500 by Saturday.

On Thursday, July 16, we were visited once again by Marie, who, after watching me do the dressing change, gave me a big thumbs up and an A plus.

Neil, a physical therapist who was also now in the picture, was also impressed with Joe.

With his appetite slowly coming back, Joe was increasing his food intake. He needed to put on some weight, and we laughed about this because Joe was always fighting the "Battle of the Bulge" for most of his adult life. Before all his heart issues began, he was at the gym four mornings a week at 5 a.m.

During one of our moments alone, he quietly said, "You know, this is only a temporary inconvenience to get me to my real goal, the heart transplant."

That statement floored me. *"Only a temporary inconvenience..."*

Joe never lost sight of his goal.

Four days after we arrived home, we returned to Columbia for follow-up visits with Dr. Mancini and the LVAD nurses. I managed to get a wheelchair for Joe in the hospital lobby, and we worked our way upstairs to see the doctor. Dr. Mancini, always stern and serious, took one look at Joe and broke out in an ear-to-ear smile. "It's great to see you," she cheerily called out. Joe handed her one of his photographs of the Brooklyn Bridge as a gift. He insisted we bring two large, framed photographs with us as gifts for Dr. Mancini and Dr. Naka. After seeing Dr. Mancini, we found our way to Dr. Naka's office but were told that he was out of town. We left the photograph of a beautiful, blazing sunset with a thank-you note.

Next, we were off to see the LVAD team. We met Margaret, the LVAD nurse manager, in the hallway while I was pushing Joe in the wheelchair. Margaret scolded him. "Joe, you have to walk! If you keep getting pushed around in a wheelchair, they're not going to consider you for a transplant. You need to walk."

"I know, Margaret," answered Joe, rather meekly, "I'm walking every day at home."

I felt my hands clench the handles of the wheelchair. I knew she meant well and was trying to encourage Joe, but I wanted to screech at her, "Give him a break! He's only been home for four days—he needs some time to get his strength back." But I didn't. Margaret had become one of Joe's strongest supporters: she just believed in tough love.

On Saturday, July 18, Joe got to see four of our grandchildren for the first time in two months. He was excited and wrote in his journal:

> Lauren and Marty brought all of the kids over. Hannah is a lot bigger and crawling. The twins are more talkative and interactive. They all played out in the yard. Kieran is the shy guy. He didn't come over to me. I guess my appearance is a bit overwhelming, but I miss giving him a big hug and kiss. Hopefully, as I get better, he'll thaw out!

It was going to be a full weekend. On Sunday, Peter and Janine were planning on visiting with their two children. Joe was rightfully excited; he had missed the kids so much during his long hospital stay. He was up early, washed and shaved and getting dressed when all of a sudden, the heart alarm on the system controller went off. Joe called out to me, and we immediately connected the white wire to the PBU to give us an indication of what was happening; everything read normal.

I called the LVAD number that we were given and was informed that a Dr. Stewart would return our call. We waited for half an hour and then called again. Another half hour went by as I paced nervously back and forth, but there was still no call back. I was beginning to panic. Even though the PBU was giving us a normal reading, I needed to have some feedback from a doctor.

We made the decision to call Dr. Naka and leave a message. He returned our call almost immediately and then told us what I, without a doubt, didn't want to hear.

"There might be a software glitch in the system controller. You need to change out the controller with the backup."

I couldn't believe what I was hearing. Even though Joe and I had been instructed about this possibility before his discharge, we were told repeatedly that it was a very rare occurrence and not to worry about it. I was trying to keep calm; after all, I was the one who had to change out the controller. I needed to show confidence even though my insides were in knots, and I was petrified.

Joe looked at me and quietly said, "We can do this together. Let's get out the directions, go over them, and then we'll start—together." Joe knew me better than anyone else on earth; he knew I was terrified, and he was trying to reassure me that I could handle this. I doubt I would have been that calm if I were in his position.

He laid down on the bed, and I opened the hand-written instructions that we had brought home from the hospital. There were thirteen steps, which we read together, going over each step one by one. When we finished, we both looked at each other and Joe asked, "Are you ready?"

"Yes," I answered feebly.

"Okay then, let's get this thing done."

The controller had to be switched out in a matter of minutes. "Help me, God," I prayed as I placed the backup controller next to Joe, ready to exchange it immediately for the original one. I kept reassuring myself, "You trained for this, Jane. You passed the quiz—you've got this." I was hoping Joe didn't see the tremor in my hands. We quickly followed each step, as I felt palpitations in my chest and sweat forming on my brow, until the new controller was hooked up and working. We didn't have much time to breathe a sigh of relief; just as we finished, Peter and his family burst into the door, the kids calling out to Papa.

At around noon, Rosie, an LVAD nurse, called to tell us that a new backup system controller would be sent by FedEx and we should receive it the next day.

The rest of the day went well and Joe wrote in his journal on Sunday, July 19:

> *I feel good again, today especially after seeing the family this weekend.*
>
> *I've got to get an exercise schedule in writing for this week.*
>
> *Another better day! Thank God for Jane and family.*

The next few days were uneventful. We were in our new normal. Joe was gaining weight and sleeping better, and I was getting quicker at doing the dressing change. He kept setting new goals for himself on the Air Life to strengthen his lungs. He was also trying to wean himself off the oxygen. Dr. Marzo called to check on Joe to wish him well: "Stay positive, Joe, and call me if you need anything." Dr. Marzo had become part of our support team.

The PT came for the last time on the 20th. Marie made her last visit on the 23rd. Everything seemed to be going well until Saturday, July 25.

At 5 a.m., the ICD fired and woke me up. This hadn't happened since November 2008, eight months before. Joe was tethered to the PBU and the display module showed all normal readings. We immediately called the LVAD team. The doctor on call told us he spoke with Dr. Naka and we were to call the team on Monday and alert them. I was shaken. I couldn't believe that Joe spent nine weeks in the hospital and the unit never fired, and here we were, not quite two weeks at home, and this happened.

Trisha, the cardiac nurse from Winthrop Hospital, called. She worked with Dr. Germano, who had implanted the ICD. They had picked up the firing on their monitor. She had spoken with Dr. Germano and filled him in, but Joe was now the patient of Drs. Naka and Mancini at Columbia. Joe wrote in his journal that night:

> *Jane is quiet. The ICD firing has upset her. I'm trying to find the answer as to why it fired. I feel it's just part of the change my body is going through and the LVAD or the ICD, or both, need to be reset. We'll see on Monday. I'm over it!*

On Sunday, Joe acted like nothing had happened. He did four laps on the deck and got to 1500 on Air Life ten times. He was off oxygen for most of the day. On this day he wrote:

> *Had a great steak dinner. (I miss a glass of wine.)*

On Monday we were back up to Columbia for a follow-up after the ICD firing. Joe's blood pressure was good, as was his oxygen level. He was put back on a beta blocker to lower his heart rate. The doctors thought his heart rate was too high, and that might have caused the arrhythmia. We were reassured not to worry about the ICD firing because the LVAD backs up the ICD. I wanted to tell them that maybe they should have been with us at 5 a.m.

Joe had a great relationship with all the LVAD nurses, but Jenn was always his favorite. All those weeks in the hospital they shared their interest in the Civil War. So on this unscheduled visit to Columbia, Joe thought enough to bring Jenn a book he thought she would enjoy. And Jenn, in return, made Joe a deal.

"Mr. B., when you get your new heart, I'll return the book."

And what was Joe's reply? "Well then, Jenn, you better read fast! "

* * *

The following days were filled with Joe setting more goals for himself and visits from family and friends, but the situation regarding the ICD firing was still not resolved. The LVAD team at Columbia wanted Joe to meet with an electrophysiologist on their staff. Joe did not want to get involved with another doctor. He called Dr. Germano and requested that he call Dr. Mancini and explain the reasons for the ICD settings. We were trying to uncomplicate our already complicated lives. On Sunday, August 2, Joe wrote:

> *Got upstairs and on the computer*
>
> *ANOTHER GOAL DONE!!*
>
> *Had dinner at Lauren and Marty's*
>
> *ANOTHER GOAL DONE!!*
>
> *Got home @ 9:30.*
>
> *To bed and reading.*
>
> *THANK GOD FOR JANE AND FAMILY*

On Monday, August 3, we were visited by some family members, including Joe's dad. That night Joe wrote this:

> *Dad was a little shocked since he thought I would look worse. I told him everything was fine and he need not worry. He's fine. He gave me rosary beads from the Vatican. My sister Jane gave me a pair of beads that belonged to my mom. Everyone left at 4:00 p.m.*
>
> *Great day!*
>
> *Thank God for Jane and family*

The next day, Joe asked me to drive him to his office. Although he was on disability, he wanted to keep up with the paperwork he had left on his desk. He got to see some of his coworkers and talk shop. This was good for him; he had worked with these people for many years, and they had become friends, not just coworkers. His goal had been to take early retirement, but the economy of 2008 squashed those dreams. Now the future was uncertain, and he was determined to keep up with what was going on in the business so that, if need be, his return to work would be an easy transition.

On the morning of Friday, August 7, Margaret called. All of Joe's blood work looked good. No changes were needed in the dosage of his meds. By this time Joe was off oxygen, and Margaret was very pleased.

In the afternoon, Joe's cousin Rosemary and her husband John visited. The next day we were going to Marty and Lauren's to celebrate Marty's birthday. On this night Joe wrote:

> Hopefully I can be reactivated on the transplant list after my next visit with Dr. Mancini on August 27.

At this time, I was working two or three days per week. Joe was beginning to feel more comfortable being left alone, and he managed to keep himself busy while I was gone. He was now hitting 1750 on the Air Life.

On Thursday, August 13, Joe began his journal with the heading "5 Weeks Home." He noted that Dr. Germano had spoken with Dr. Mancini's NP and explained the ICD settings to her. We were hopeful that this would be the end of it.

Joe was still looking into photography competitions and submitting his work. He was always scanning the internet for new shows coming up, sending out letters and samples of his work to local waterfront restaurants, hoping to interest them in displaying his photography. He already had one local eatery interested, and the owner gave him a list of local sites they wished to have photographed. Once he became strong enough, he ventured out on his own to take the pictures. He would not allow the LVAD to hold him back. He was looking forward to, and planning for, the future.

By August 19 Joe had met his goal of 2000 on Air Life and was now working with hand weights. Things seemed to be moving along well, but on Friday, August 21 we had another scare. Joe wrote:

> Up @ 9 a.m.—weight 175 lbs.
>
> System controller beeped 1X when I was standing in my bedroom. Speed and PI #s dropped, 8160 and 4.0, respectively. Flow ——- No message on display panel. Jane called LVAD and spoke with

Jenn. She said log shows speed and PI had dropped that low in the past, and this could have been caused by not taking in enough liquids. That could be true because yesterday I only drank about 40 ozs. Not enough.

It's 11:30 a.m. I feel fine.

Jane ran into her office and the bank. She'll stay home with me today—That makes me feel better! I'm really glad she's home today

Thank God for Jane and that she's OK.

The last reference was to my visit with a kidney doctor. I was trying to keep up with my own health, knowing that Joe needed me and would need me even more after the transplant. I saw Dr. Curran for my annual physical. Some protein showed up in my bloodwork, and he, never an alarmist but always cautionary, thought it would be a good idea to check it out further.

I didn't give it much thought; I felt fine and wouldn't let myself go into that dark place of questioning, *could something be wrong with me?* Joe and I didn't discuss it much. There were too many other things going on, and the problems with Joe were staring us in the face every day. Being hooked up to a machine doesn't let you forget, even for a second, the severity of what's happening, so I made the appointment with the kidney doctor, who sent me for a battery of tests. After the results came back, he concluded that my kidney function, although not exactly where it should be, was good. That certainly was great news to me and apparently to Joe, who it seemed was worried more than I thought.

August 27 finally arrived, and we made our way up to Columbia for Joe's follow-up visit. This was the appointment Joe had been waiting for. He was doing well, feeling stronger, and hoping he would be reactivated on the transplant list. He was anticipating getting on the list again, looking forward to moving on and enjoying life. We both got some good news that day. Joe noted:

Dr. Mancini all smiles! Very happy with everything. She wants to reactivate me on the A1 list, but Dr. Naka is in Japan, so she wants to wait until next week when he returns

Reactivation will put me in a high-priority position on the list for 30 days

Went to dinner with Jane and stopped at Lauren and Marty's. A good day!

Thank God for Jane

On August 31 Joe mentioned he had trimmed the bushes out front, even though we had a landscaper. He also wrote:

Tomorrow I'm driving to town for a haircut. First time driving since May 7, 2009

On Tuesday, September 9, he entered in his journal:

Went to town—drove. YIPPEE!!!

In the weeks Joe had been home from Columbia, all we tried to do was live our lives as best as we could. We knew what our ultimate goal was, the transplant, but we never really discussed it. At this point, we were just trying to get Joe stronger so he would be ready when the call did come. We both thought that would take months, so we concentrated on each day, thankful that he was home.

I had missed him so much when he was in the hospital. Each day, walking into an empty house was depressing and frightening. I couldn't imagine my life without Joe. Having been together since our teenage years, the thought of losing him unnerved me, so I focused on his getting stronger. Joe was the toughest guy I knew. I reminded myself several times a day that if anyone could get through this, it would be him.

During all those weeks of waiting, Joe showed nothing but confidence. He concentrated on keeping up with things at work, enjoying the visitors who continually dropped by, worked on his photography, played with the grandkids, and looked forward to future events. He had some kind of plan for each day; sitting around and feeling sorry for himself was not an option. The stronger he got the busier he made himself.

On Wednesday, September 2, he wrote:

O2 company picked up tanks and O2 machine @ 6:45 p.m. I'm glad to see them gone and hope we don't get them back ever.

In all the years we were married, Joe never forgot an anniversary or birthday. With all that was happening, on Thursday, September 3, he wrote in his journal that he went into town for an anniversary card for me. On Friday, September 4, he wrote:

Today would have been Danny's 58th B-Day—Miss you!

Happy Birthday, Dawg.

Even with all the tussles of the older and younger brother growing up together, neither Joe nor Danny ever forgot each other's birthdays.

On Saturday, September 5, Joe wrote in big, bold letters

JACK'S 7th B-DAY!!

On Sunday, September 6, he wrote:

HANNAH'S FIRST BIRTHDAY!!

On Monday, September 7, he wrote

Our 41st anniversary!

He wrote about our babysitting Hannah for the day and walking around the lake, about half a mile. He was getting stronger and feeling better each day. He was out doing photo shoots and editing his pictures. He was now up to 2250 on Air Life. Even though he was still attached to the LVAD, life seemed almost ordinary. We were enjoying these days, having fun with the kids, going out to dinner, and living like everyone else.

I don't know how Joe felt, but I was grateful for the routine. I had him back, and between bandage changes, sponge baths, lab work, meds, and visits to Columbia, we were enjoying life. He was here with me, holding my hand, eating dinner and taking walks with me. It was a new way of life for us, but I was grateful for it. I knew that when the transplant happened, it would be a whole new journey, and the unknown terrified me. These days were numbered, and I was trying to hold on to them for as long as possible.

A few days after our anniversary, Joe presented me with a small box from Tiffany's. "I'm sorry this is late."

"How did you manage to buy me a gift?" I asked.

"Internet," he said with a smile. "I just couldn't get it here for our actual anniversary." This man continued to amaze me.

As I read the entries in Joe's journal from during those days of waiting, the key factor was that they were all positive. He focused on the everyday activities of a man with a future, a man filled with happiness over the commonplace joys of life: grandchildren, family members, friends.

He mentioned taking the car in for maintenance and going to Ace Hardware to pick up three leader extensions and some seed and fertilizer. He wrote about a visit from his boss, talking with neighbors, buying flowers, printing a special black-and-white photo for a family member, getting an estimate on landscape lighting, finally getting back to church, and Dr. Marzo's invitation to participate in his patient talent show in November. He commented on my preparing a pot roast dinner and our dining by candlelight. He added,

"A glass of red wine would have been nice. I'll wait!"

He never once gave any indication that he was worried about things not going well, even though he had been through so much after receiving the LVAD. His mental state, now that I think back, was quite remarkable. I saw no depression in him. If he had fears, he kept them to himself.

He did give a lot of thought to those whom he thought gave him inspiration. With that in mind, he wrote his essay **Heroes** and sent it out to family and friends.

HEROES—*September 13, 2009*

Almost all of us need a hero, or heroes, in our lives. People to get us through a normal day or through a major event in our life.

A hero is someone you can look at and use what they did or are doing with their lives to help you get through whatever simple or complicated event you are experiencing.

The event that I am experiencing is well known to all of you, and thus the need for me to have heroes to help me get through "The Journey." My first hero is my brother Danny. Danny passed away just three years ago this month, about three weeks after his 55th birthday. He had a nasty form of lymphoma, and we were preparing for a bone marrow transplant, since I matched with him. He did not make it to that procedure, but he fought like hell to beat the disease right up to the end. He always had an upbeat attitude during his struggle, kept his sense of humor through his battle, and stayed positive the whole time. I guess in the end God didn't want him to suffer any longer and took him to a better place.

Danny's struggle has taught me to fight, battle, to stay strong during "The Journey," and when I get down, I can hear him saying, "What up, Dawg?" I respond in my mind, "I'm UP, Dawg, stay with me, help me, and I miss you." I know he's with me. I feel his presence.

The rest of my heroes are not in any order of importance, so here goes.

My son-in-law, Marty, is a hero to me. When Marty was about 23, he was diagnosed with Hodgkin's disease. At first he questioned: WHY? Why would a healthy young man develop such a disease? He fought and battled his disease, listening to his doctor's instruction and advice, doing whatever needed to be done to defeat his Hodgkin's disease. I believe that he never gave up for a second, and with the support of his family and friends, he beat his disease and has remained cancer free. Marty is a caring, giving, and loving man who is helping my daughter, Lauren, raise four of my six beautiful grandchildren. He has been with Jane and I through my struggle, and he knows that "The Journey" will have a successful conclusion. Marty, I love you, man!

My next hero, or in this case heroes, are the men and women of our armed forces, especially those fighting in Iraq and Afghanistan.

During my nine weeks in the hospital, May through July, simple, everyday things that all of us take for granted, were not so simple. Going to the bathroom, shaving, brushing my teeth, showering, getting out of bed, walking, eating, etc., were difficult for me without some kind of assistance. If I started to feel sorry for myself or down, I thought of those brave people, thousands of miles away from their families, and their inability to shower every day, eat normal food, go to a normal bathroom, shave daily, etc. And along with all of this, they're being shot at. Since they were not feeling sorry for their situation, there was no way I was going to get down on myself. Appreciating whatever I could do for myself, with or without assistance, became something that made me stronger each day. It gave me a goal to be able to do those everyday things by myself, and thank all those people—family and hospital staff who were helping me to recover. And no one was shooting at me!

We need to, in our own way, THANK those brave men and women for what they do for this country.

Larry Callahan is the son of a good friend of ours who lives outside of San Francisco. In 1994 Larry contracted a virus which left him a quadriplegic. Larry was 22 years old at the time. I spent some time with Larry when we visited San Francisco, and we seemed to click. He was an avid reader, listened to talk radio, and had a wonderful perception and insight as to what was going on politically in the country. He kept himself informed on current events. We recommended various books to each other, spoke on the phone, and exchanged emails.

Larry's day was spent either in bed or in a wheelchair, which he controlled with a tube in his mouth. He was able to go to the movies with the help of his younger brother, Gerard, or his mother, Lorraine. There was no cure for the virus that had paralyzed him, and he had constant visits by nurses and physical therapists. There were also hospital stays to treat the infections that occurred and other problems brought on by his condition.

Larry, like my brother Danny, was a fighter. I don't think he ever felt sorry for himself; he lived his life as if it were God's plan for him. When his condition worsened, he said to his mother, "If anything happens to me, I want Joe to have my heart." Lorraine explained to Larry that they lived too far away for that to happen and not to give it any more thought. When I heard that story, I cried. Here was someone who had been stricken with a deadly virus that took away his freedom, his youth, and a normal life but still had another person in mind that he felt he needed to help.

Larry's courage, strength, and attitude make him another of my heroes.

Larry Callahan lost his fight on July 29, 2009, at the age of 37. God bless you, Larry. You're always in my prayers.

Last but not least is someone who never saw herself as a hero, but my wife of 41 years, Jane, has gone above and beyond the call, caring for me. Caring for me is not an easy job. I am not the type of person who likes to be waited on or mothered, but Jane waits on me and mothers me just the same. The first couple of weeks *at home were a struggle until I gradually started doing things for myself. Not that Jane did those things wrong, I just made it my goal to have less for her to do and more for me to do on my own in order to get back to "normal."*

*She has given me a tremendous amount of physical and mental support, and I **will** reward all of her efforts and love with a successful completion of "The Journey."*

Jane—I love you, always!

I also have love and thanks for my son, Peter, his wife, Janine, my daughter Lauren, and her husband, Marty, for forming what I call my "Team of Angels," along with Jane. They each took up a different role, now and when I was hospitalized, to basically shield me from the day-to-day distractions that you need to avoid so you can get on with getting better: medical forms, doctors forms, insurance claims, things that needed to be done at home, etc., and just their constant love and support got me on the road to recovery.

Lastly . . . a giant THANK YOU to all of my relatives, friends, co-workers and neighbors who have been with me on every step of "The Journey."

I feel I am close to a successful end to "The Journey," and then I can continue on with what I want to do and enjoy all those things life has to offer. Thank you all for being there. May God bless each and every one of you.

CHAPTER FIFTEEN

WAITING IS HARD WORK

While Joe was hooked up to the BiVAD, his spirits were good. We never discussed the failed transplant; we just spoke about him getting stronger for the second heart. We couldn't allow negativity to creep into our lives. Our focus needed to be on the prize, and we tried to concentrate on that each day.

But as tough and positive as he tried to be, at times Joe got down. Who could blame him after all he had been through?

The last tube was taken out of his chest on October 18. He was tired that day and didn't feel like walking with Dave. It was the first indication that the strong exterior Joe always showed was starting to crack.

I noticed some changes; he just wasn't his usual self. I advised him to ask Margaret for a low dose of an antidepressant. We needed to nip this in the bud.

"You can't handle everything on your own," I told him. "You've already proven how strong you are, but sometimes everyone needs a little help."

Margaret suggested that Joe talk to the psychiatrist and, surprisingly, he agreed. After a consultation, the psychiatrist concluded that Joe didn't need any medication at this time for depression. I totally disagreed. One fifteen-minute consultation with a patient, in my opinion, wasn't enough to provide information for a diagnosis of mental fitness. I knew Joe better than anyone else, and I definitely saw a change in his demeanor. I kept wondering if this doctor knew Joe's history, of all that he had gone through, not only in the past few months at Columbia but for the nine years leading up to this. How could anyone endure such ups and downs, all the euphoria and disappointments, and not be depressed? Joe carried himself very well, though his pride sometimes got in the way of common sense. I was determined to get him some help. *Screw the psychiatrist*, I told myself as I reached out to Dr. Mancini.

At times I just wanted to tell Joe, "It's okay to be scared. It's okay to feel like you got shafted. It's okay to question *why me?*"

But I never did because I knew that Joe would never let his guard down. Sometimes I think he was still trying to protect me.

After some discussion, Dr. Mancini put him on an antidepressant.

On October 23 I arrived at the hospital at my usual time. As I approached Joe's room, I was greeted by a group of doctors surrounding Joe's bed and a nurse telling me to wait outside. "What's happening?" I shouted.

Margaret approached, and then I saw Peter coming toward me. I was beside myself. "Mom, Dad's heart rate shot up to 278; the cardiac team rushed in."

I felt weak in the knees. Margaret kept reassuring me. "Jane, he's protected by the BiVAD; his heart rate doesn't mean anything."

I asked, "Then how come the cardiac team rushed in?"

It turned out Margaret was right—neither Dr. Naka nor Dr. Mancini gave orders for drugs. They both insisted the BiVAD was doing its job. Joe and I were on a roller coaster ride and neither one of us, even when we were kids, liked roller coasters.

The next day everything was back to our new normal. Considering what had happened, Joe looked well. His heart rate was back to a stable 140, and he was surprised with a visit from one of his nephews.

On Sunday, October 25, his cousin's pastor, who was visiting one of her parishioners at the hospital, stopped by to say hello to Joe. Peter came to see his dad and brought him a sandwich from Hoboken—always a treat. Joe called Lauren's and spoke to the kids. He became emotional when he handed me back the phone. This was difficult for all of us, and the waiting was getting to be torturous.

But the next day, our patience was finally rewarded.

CHAPTER SIXTEEN

A Second Chance

October 26 was a beautiful, cloudless day. Frank, Marty's dad, visited with Father Dan, our former pastor. Father Dan prayed with us, not only for Joe but for all the doctors and nurses who gave so much care and comfort to the sick at Columbia. He administered the Anointing of the Sick to Joe, and we all received Holy Communion. It was a beautiful few moments, and both Joe and I were touched.

Frank and Father Dan went to the waiting area to appreciate the beautiful view of the Hudson River when a bevy of nurses stormed into the room. "Mr. B., did you eat your lunch?"

"No, not yet," Joe answered.

"Great," they exclaimed as they whisked away the untouched meal and informed us there was a potential heart that could possibly match with Joe. When Father Dan and Frank came back into the room and heard the news, Joe, his usual self, quipped,

"Wow, Fr. Dan, you really work fast!"

Joe and I started our long wait. All antigens had to be cross-checked, which, we were informed, would take hours. All four of the LVAD nurses came in to hug us and wish us good luck before they went home. By 9:30

p.m. we were told it would probably be a go, and they would take Joe down around 12:30 a.m. Both Peter and Lauren arrived by 11:00.

As the nurses changed shifts, each came to wish us luck. A few of them took me aside to tell me how amazing Joe was, how strong and positive he remained, and what a wonderful patient he had been. They reassured me that he deserved this heart, and it would happen.

The time kept changing, but finally, at 3:30 a.m., we said goodbye to Joe. As he was being wheeled to the OR, all the nurses at the station held up their arms displaying their GO JOE wristbands and in unison chanted, "Go Joe! Go Joe!"

The next hours were very, very long, and both my children and I were dealing with our own personal thoughts and fears. At one point, Jenn informed us that Joe was still on bypass, so it would be a few more hours. At 9:30 a.m. I spotted Dr. Naka coming toward me. To say I held my breath is an understatement, but he caught my eye, and I saw a smile form on his lips. "Mrs. Bavoso," he said when he reached me, "it was a really good heart, and I'm very pleased. Everything went perfectly."

I was so happy to see that Dr. Naka had performed the surgery. I had a feeling that after the first failed transplant Dr. Naka wanted to be involved in the second surgery. Peter and Janine, Lauren and Marty, and I collapsed into each other's arms. We cried openly, but this time they were tears of joy. When we entered that waiting room, I had nothing but bad memories, and just sitting there was torture, but now we were one of those happy families. It was our turn to get some good news.

* * *

We were allowed to see Joe in recovery and were advised that he was still under sedation but doing well. I walked slowly to the ICU. The memory of three weeks ago and the first transplant was still fresh in my mind, and although my hopes were high, I still didn't know what to expect. When I finally reached the room, I stood at the door and looked around. *Where is all the equipment?* I thought to myself. A few IV bags hung from a pole and a monitor was next to the bed keeping track of his heart rate, but that was about it. I gazed at Joe and thought he looked nothing like he had after the first transplant. Peter spoke first. "Mom, we can actually get near the bed and hold his hand!"

A young nurse stood next to the bed, monitoring him.

"He's doing remarkably well!" she said cheerily. "I took care of Mr. B. during my night shifts. I really got to know him, and I was here last night when he was taken to surgery, so I requested to stay on duty this morning to take care of him post-op. He is such a great guy, and I had to be here with him after he got his heart. He was an amazing patient. Congratulations! I'm so happy for everyone!"

As we walked out of the room, many nurses who had taken care of Joe over the past couple of months came running over to hug us and offer their congratulations. As we walked through the lobby of the hospital on our way home, Paris the security guard ran over and hugged Peter and then me as he yelled loudly, "Go, Joe!"

I arrived home exhausted but elated. I silently spoke to God. "It was a long road, with plenty of twists and turns but we're here. Thank you. Please, continue to give us strength."

I was always a prayerful person, but in all those days I don't remember praying formally as we Catholics often do with our novenas, rosaries, and Masses. I didn't have the strength, so I just had conversations with the Almighty. I knew through all the emails I had received from family and friends, plus all the prayer and Mass cards that were sent to us, that plenty of formal prayers were being said for Joe every day.

The next day, Thursday, October 29, when Lauren and I walked back into the ICU, Joe was sitting up in bed and talking. "So, how are you doing today?" he asked me with a smile.

"Pretty good. But the real question is, how are you doing?"

"Great," he answered.

He had been taken off the ventilator at 10:30 a.m., and all his numbers were good. Both of us were grinning from ear to ear. Dr. Farr, the cardiologist, came in and assured us that everything was going well. She advised Joe that his ticket out of the hospital was to have no infections and three negative biopsies. Rejection was now the worry we were facing. The first biopsy was scheduled for Monday. This would continue weekly for months to catch any rejection early and so the doctors could adjust his anti-rejection meds. Of course, Joe asked about the grandkids and when he would be able to see them.

"How old are they?" Dr. Farr inquired.

"Seven, five, four and a half, two-year-old twins, and a one-year-old," Joe answered without hesitation.

"Whew, that's quite a crew," Dr. Farr laughed. "Well, Joe, the three oldest can visit with masks and rubber gloves, but the three youngest will have to wait for a few months. Infection is the enemy, and children are breeders of germs."

I saw the disappointment on Joe's face, but Lauren piped in, "Dad, it's only for a few months. Just think, once you're cleared, you'll be able to see them for the next twenty years."

He was tired from all the monitoring during the night and looked a little puffy from the steroids he was receiving. The good news was that his ejection fraction (the pumping of the heart) was at 59 percent, an incredible increase from the 25 percent before the first transplant. Dr. Farr said this would get even better with time.

The first goal was to get Joe out of the ICU by the next day so they could get him walking. Dave was standing by, ready to get Joe into action. After checking Joe's arms and legs, Dave declared that they were strong. Joe was ready for his next step.

Recipient families are never given much information about the donor, but I finally learned Joe's heart came from a twenty-five-year-old male from Westchester County. As happy as I was, I thought of this young man and his family and asked God to welcome him home and grant his family peace and strength. It really was a mixed bag of emotions.

CHAPTER SEVENTEEN

THE HOME STRETCH

Numerous hospital stays over the previous nine years for a defibrillator implant, an ablation, and various other incidents, plus nine weeks in the hospital after receiving the LVAD followed by two heart transplants, made us both truly believe that we were now in the home stretch.

All it would take was three negative biopsies. *We're almost there, God—help us get to the finish line.* I recited those words each day on my return trip. The doctors kept reassuring us that Joe was doing great. They seemed as excited and happy as we were. No one likes to fail, and a hospital as large as NY Columbia Presbyterian certainly didn't want the scourge of a failed transplant on its excellent record, so everyone was ecstatic about Joe's progress. He was experiencing some stomach issues, but that was inevitable because he was now on a long list of medications. We were reassured that eventually, his system would adjust.

On October 30, Dr. Naka, the transplant surgeon, stopped by telling Joe somewhat kiddingly, "Hey, maybe by next week, you'll be home." I cringed when he said that because Joe was hanging on to every word, and I knew that that wasn't in the cards. There were still lines and tubes in Joe's chest, and he was just now able to sit in a chair for a short time.

On November 2 he was moved to a coronary care unit, the next phase before a step-down unit. Joe was getting stronger, and on this day his last chest tube and the IV line were finally removed. He wasn't tethered anymore! Joe never complained, but I couldn't imagine feeling tied to something for as many times and for as long as he had been—first the LVAD, then the BiVAD, and now all the lines and tubes. Joe was a man of little patience, but he seemed never to lose patience with all of this paraphernalia attached to him. He just accepted it as part of this journey he was on. On November 3, I wrote in my journal: "*I stayed home today—I think I have finally hit the wall.*" I was totally exhausted, both physically and mentally.

I wasn't there when Joe was moved to the step-down unit. On this exciting day, he walked with Dave and used the bathroom "like a man," as Joe described it. His first biopsy was taken, and the numbers were looking good. When Joe got back from the testing, he was moved to a private room, thanks again to our friends. I was hoping this would finally allow him to get the rest and sleep he desperately needed.

On November 4 Lauren visited Joe with me. Joe looked good, but he was getting agitated by all the bloodwork and testing that was being done. The steroids he was on, which can cause agitation, were starting to kick in, which was quite apparent on another day when I arrived at the hospital. As I approached the room, I saw a man I didn't recognize standing at the foot of Joe's bed. When I entered, Peter, who had gotten there before me, caught my eye and gave me a strange look. The man introduced himself as a heart transplant recipient six years earlier. He looked so healthy and strong that it immediately gave me hope for Joe. The gentleman had stopped by to give us all some moral support and Joe seemed to be on a rant. He was speaking nonstop, telling the visitor all about his plans to make the public more aware of organ donation.

"I'm a marketing guy; I've got plenty of ideas swirling around in my head," Joe spouted. "When I'm on my feet again, I'm going to meet with Dr. Schulman, and we're going to go over some of my ideas. I'm also starting to outline a book about this experience. One of the cardiologists offered his help with the medical part. I'm going to be writing about the psychological and emotional part. I also started a small photography business, and I want to expand on that."

Joe just kept talking and talking. He explained he was a Civil War buff and planned on visiting all the battlegrounds of the War as well as all the national parks. His list was endless, and this poor man, who had visited to give moral support, stood there and listened. I could now understand the strange look Peter had given me.

Joe was always a good conversationalist. Being an avid reader, he could pretty much hold his own on almost any topic, but he never monopolized a conversation or was rude. So I was thinking, *what's wrong with him*?

When the gentleman ended the visit, we thanked him for his time and for sharing his experience. Peter had to get back to his office, so I walked with him to the elevator. "What was that all about?" I queried.

"Mom, Dad's on really heavy doses of steroids. Obviously, they're kicking in," Peter said. "I think Mr. Grant realized that. He went through the same thing. As the doctors start to decrease Dad's dosage, he'll calm down."

Wow, I thought. *What a ride we're on.*

A second biopsy was taken on November 10 and it came back negative. We were on cloud nine.

November 16 found me at home, cleaning the house for Joe's homecoming. He was scheduled to have his last biopsy that day, and if everything went well, he would be released two days later. Infection was such a big factor that I wanted everything to be almost sterile. Although I desperately wanted Joe home, I was also becoming stressed because I would once again be solely responsible for his well-being.

Dr. Mancini was trying her best to keep him for another week. Joe had gone through so much, and in her wisdom, she felt that another week in the hospital would give him more rest and more time for observation. Joe was becoming adamant about going home, and there really wasn't any reason—other than caution—to keep him. The final biopsy also came back negative, and on Wednesday, November 18, Joe finally came home with his new heart!

Lauren and I went to pick him up from Columbia. He was sitting on the side of the bed, all dressed and ready to go when we entered his room, just about "chomping at the bit" to leave. Paperwork had to be completed before release, and every hospital seems to take forever to get all that together.

Joe was more distressed than usual and was giving me grief over administrative issues I couldn't control. Lauren stepped out of the room and ran into Margaret.

"How's your dad doing?" she asked.

"Well, right now he's giving my mom a hard time," Lauren told her. "He wants to get out of here ASAP, but his paperwork isn't ready yet, so he's really agitated."

"Steroids," Margaret answered knowingly. "I'll handle this."

The next thing I knew, she was in the room.

"Good morning, Joe! Very exciting—it's going home day! Now, I want to tell you something. You are under no circumstances to give Jane a hard time. She has no control over paperwork, and I want you to remember one very important thing. Jane is your lifeline and caretaker. When you go home, you're going to need her more than ever. If I were you, I would be really nice to my wife. That's an order!"

For the first time in days, Joe remained silent.

The paperwork was finally finished, and an orderly arrived with a wheelchair to take Joe downstairs. Khristine, the LVAD nurse we had met months before, seemed to pop up out of nowhere. "Uh, uh—no one's taking Mr. B. downstairs but me," she cheerfully announced.

And so Khristine escorted us downstairs. Upon arriving in the lobby, Paris, who had been so supportive of all of us during these long months, ran over and hugged both Lauren and me and then Joe. "God bless you, sir. You have a remarkable family. I wish you nothing but health and happiness."

It was a good sendoff from Columbia.

As we exited the parkway, I told Joe to look to his right. At the bottom of the ramp, a huge sign read, **"GO JOE—Welcome Home."** Lauren had placed it there the night before. When we arrived at our house, red heart balloons greeted us with a big welcome home sign.

I helped Joe out of the car, but before he would go into the house, he asked me to take a picture of him with all the balloons.

I was happy to oblige.

CHAPTER EIGHTEEN

THE FIRST DAY

November 19 was Joe's first full day home. He slept for twenty hours. *"When you rest, you heal,"* was my journal entry. I had to wake him to give him his drugs; he was adamant about not getting up. Joe was exhausted and wanted nothing more than to sleep.

He had always taken care of his own medications, but now he seemed to have no interest in keeping track of this himself. Steroids were changing his personality, so the responsibility fell on me. Every day I filled the daily pill box provided by Columbia. Both of us were instructed as to what each drug was for, the dosage, the time of day to take each drug, etc. There were twenty-two different medications.

Our daily routine began with checking his blood pressure, which was at a stable 132/84, his heart rate always between 96 and 108, his weight holding at 173 pounds, and finally his temperature, a normal 98.6. We would breathe a sigh of relief when all his vitals were good and I would jot the numbers down in a book.

On November 21, Joe attempted to go upstairs. He couldn't do it. The hematoma he experienced after the first transplant was still not healed, and his leg was weak. What we did accomplish that day was getting Joe in the shower. It was his first one since May 11. It took so much of his energy and so much of my strength that I don't think he really enjoyed it, but it was a victory to me.

On November 24 we had our first outpatient visit. Another biopsy was required. We were up at 5 a.m. Upon our arrival, both of us were happy to see Dr. Farr. She was a naturally attractive woman, tall and thin with long blonde hair and a beautiful smile. The first time Joe met her, she walked into his room while he was on the phone with a friend. He joked with his pal, "Sorry, I have to go. The most beautiful woman just walked into my room, and I'd much rather speak with her than you." So we were happily surprised when we saw Dr. Farr on Joe's first outpatient visit.

"You look great, Joe," she greeted us in a pleasant voice. After her exam she asked, "Any questions?"

"Dr. Farr," Joe started, "can I go to my daughter's for Thanksgiving dinner? I won't stay long. Just for dinner so I can see my grandchildren, and then I'll go home. I haven't seen them in such a long time."

I think that Dr. Farr, hearing the yearning in Joe's voice, felt she had no other choice but to give in to Joe's request with another warning.

"You know, Joe, children are the biggest carriers of germs. Promise me you'll wear a mask and try to get the children to wear one too. Make it a game. Have them draw pictures or faces on the mask and then put it on. I know you want to, but you can't let them sit on your lap or kiss you. This is going to be difficult, but we definitely want to avoid infection."

"I promise," answered Joe. "I'll follow the rules. Just give me permission to go."

On November 25, the day before Thanksgiving, we received a call from the hospital telling us that Joe's white cell count was very low.

I spoke with a nurse I didn't know, telling her that Joe's temperature was 99.3.

She told me he needed a shot of Neupogen to increase his white blood cell count. "You don't have to come into the hospital," she said. "You can give him the shot yourself."

"I could never do that," I answered, "but I do have a few friends who are nurses. They'd gladly come over and give Joe the shot."

And so that day my friend Barbara came over. And even though she didn't say anything, as a trained nurse I'm sure she knew Joe didn't look very good.

On November 26, Thanksgiving Day, Joe had no desire or ability to go to Lauren's, no matter how much he was looking forward to it. Lauren brought us dinner, but Joe was feeling too awful to eat. I took his temperature again; it was now 101.2. I put a call into the hospital, and they put me in touch with a Dr. Jorde. He told me to get Joe to the hospital immediately. And so, on Thanksgiving night, just eight days after we came home, we were on our way back to Columbia.

Lauren drove. I don't remember a single word being spoken in the car. What was there to say? We had just left the hospital with fanfare, and now we were on our way back. I can't even imagine what was going through Joe's mind, but I knew what was going through mine—fear. Absolute fear.

We were directed to the ER, which was startling to me. Over the past three weeks we had been continuously cautioned about infection. We had received flowers and fruit baskets from friends that we couldn't keep because flowers and fresh fruit can have bacteria that would not be harmful to an average, healthy person but could be deadly to a heart transplant recipient. I had purchased a new vacuum that was guaranteed to destroy any allergens in the carpet. The house was spotless from top to bottom. I scrubbed potatoes with soap and water, as instructed, before I peeled them, to rid the skin of any bacteria that could be transferred to the potato. Eggs were banned, as was salad. The list seemed endless, and yet here we were in the general population of the ER in a large New York City hospital on a holiday night. Joe was set up in a small cubicle with oxygen and a heart monitor. The young

ER resident on call came in asking what I thought under the circumstances were unnecessary and ridiculous questions. So I asked, "You do know that my husband is a heart transplant recipient, don't you?"

"Yes," was his reply.

"He's running a temperature and Dr. Jorde instructed us to get him to the hospital immediately."

"I'm aware of that, but he has to go through the ER before we can admit him."

"He's only been home eight days, he needs to get up to the cardiac unit," I answered frantically.

"Well, we can't do that until all the paperwork is filled out here."

I wanted to scream, *Are you crazy? Get him the hell out of this petri dish of germs and infection.* But no matter what I said, we just sat there. This young doctor kept coming in and out of the cubicle asking Joe how he felt and checking his vitals. He was treating Joe as any other ER patient. He didn't seem to know what to do.

"Please call upstairs to the cardiac care unit. He needs to get there immediately," I pleaded.

My words were ignored. It wasn't until 5 a.m. on November 27 that Joe was finally transferred to the CCU.

When we saw Dr. Jorde, he told me that he was surprised Joe was not on a ventilator. I was shocked at that statement. A ventilator? He continued, telling me that most heart transplant patients who return to the hospital with a fever are usually put on a ventilator. Dr. Jorde said this was a good sign.

On November 28, his dad's ninety-third birthday, we were told that Joe had an infection and pneumonia. He was listed as critical. My heart sank. We had come so far.

I wrote in my journal about the time between Sunday, November 29, and Thursday, December 3:

Joe feeling awful. Infection under control. Heart in irregular
rhythm—kidneys starting to come back. Joe very depressed, and
steroids doing a job on him. I'm so tired—will this ever be over
so we can just enjoy the joy of a new heart? I beg God every day
to help Joe. I pray to Mary and St. Jude. He's come so far. I miss
him so much. I need him home. God, watch over Joe.

Joe was taken off the anti-rejection drugs to give his white cell count a chance to increase, which caused the heart to go into an irregular rhythm. There was no sign of rejection at this point, but another biopsy was scheduled to be done in a day or two. His kidneys were also affected by the sudden drop of his blood pressure and were not functioning properly. The good thing was that Joe was still breathing well on his own.

The doctors were encouraging and told us that by the following week they hoped to have Joe out of the CCU and walking. They were pretty certain that he would be home for Christmas, although he would be on antibiotics for weeks to come.

Christmas was looming ahead of us. Joe loved Christmas, and now that we had grandchildren, he loved it even more. We had already missed Thanksgiving; it just wasn't fair. *Give him a break God, I prayed. Please let him be home for Christmas.*

Christmas 1968 was our first Christmas together as a married couple. It was also the year that the Hong Kong Flu reared its ugly head, and Joe was one of its victims. After being married just three months and adjusting to being a wife, I was now learning how to be a caretaker. Joe was flat on his back, running a high temperature. I had to help him out of bed so I could change the sweat-soaked sheets and help him into dry pajamas. Christmas was a week away, and our plans for buying our first tree together changed into my cousin coming with me and helping me drag it up the four flights of stairs to Joe's and my three-room apartment. I managed to decorate the small spruce the best I could. I was hoping Joe would be better so we could make it to Christmas dinner at my parent's house. I couldn't imagine not being with my family on Christmas Day.

Christmas morning came, and I walked into the small living room and turned on the tree lights. I spied two small packages with my name on them, wrapped in Christmas paper and tied up in red bows.

I turned to Joe, who had followed me into the room. "When did you ever buy these gifts?"

"I picked up some small things for you before I got sick. I'm sorry; I planned on doing more shopping."

"That's okay," I told him. "This is perfect."

We made it to my parent's house that day, just like Joe had promised.

CHAPTER NINETEEN

EVERYTHING STARTS TO SLIP

The day after Joe was admitted to the CCU, Dr. Farr came in to check on him. "Mrs. Bavoso, I'm so sorry this happened. I wish you had brought him to the hospital immediately when he had a low-grade fever."

"Dr. Farr," I answered, "that was the first thing I asked when I spoke with the nurse who called about the low white cell count. She insisted it wasn't necessary, that he just needed an injection of Neupogen. A friend of mine gave him that the same day."

"That nurse told me that you said you couldn't come because you had no one to bring him to the hospital. I told her that Joe Bavoso had more friends than anyone I knew."

"Dr. Farr," I quietly answered, "he had me."

"I know, Mrs. Bavoso, and I also knew she was lying. I can guarantee she will never work in this unit again. I'm so sorry."

After a week in the CCU, Joe seemed to be responding to the antibiotics. Dr. Tsiouris, an infectious disease doctor, now entered the picture. He was trying to find out exactly what type of bacteria was causing the infection so he could treat it accordingly.

Dr. Mancini stopped by, and that always made Joe and me feel better. In her no-nonsense, professional way, we knew she had everything under control, and because of that, we felt safe and calm. She was very encouraging and told us she hoped to have Joe out of the CCU and walking the following week. She, like the other doctors, said that if all continued to go well, Joe should be home for Christmas. I think she threw that in to give us something positive to look forward to. We needed some hope. The days ahead proved to be challenging, and things changed from hour to hour. Because of the infection, Joe's blood pressure dropped dangerously low, which caused his kidneys to go into shock. We now had a kidney specialist involved again. He felt it was a temporary situation and that in a few days the kidneys would "wake up," as he put it.

The disappointment of being back in the hospital so quickly became overwhelming to Joe. That worried all of us because his attitude and goal-setting is what had gotten him through the past months.

Some news from that week helped somewhat. Another biopsy was taken and again showed no rejection. I thought of this as a gift; Joe had been off the anti-rejection drugs since being admitted to the hospital almost two weeks earlier. The kidney doctor informed me outside Joe's room that the kidneys were performing very well. I told this very kind nephrologist how despondent Joe had become, and without hesitation he said, "I'll talk to him myself." He reassured Joe that everything was going well and to just hang in there.

Dr. Mancini stopped by once more and was confident that although this turn of events was challenging, everything was going in the right direction. Joe's reply to her was that he didn't want to "crash and burn." That brought tears to my eyes, but she again reassured him that it wouldn't happen.

I had been sending out emails to family and friends since this journey began, and I continued to do so. When I updated everyone about the current situation, I added a request.

Some of you have told me that when Joe came home you took your "GO JOE" bracelet off, thinking the journey was over, but you put it back on when he was readmitted to the hospital. Sorry, but as always, I have a request. Please, please keep wearing your bracelet. It gives me some comfort knowing that if you look down and see the bracelet, it will remind you to say a prayer or think positive thoughts for Joe. This journey is far from over—now let's all just pray that Joe comes home soon. GO JOE!!!!!

* * *

When the doctors felt Joe was stable enough, they released him from the CCU and sent him to a cardiac floor. Although we were thrilled, we were also disappointed that he wasn't sent back to the seventh floor where all this started. He had spent so many weeks in that unit that we had gotten to know the staff well and felt it would be an easier transition for all of us to go back to a familiar place. Instead, Joe was sent to the fifth floor.

This proved unfortunate for us all.

CHAPTER TWENTY

BACK TO THE BEGINNING

I was again traveling to Columbia every day, but this time I saw a big difference in the attitude of the fifth-floor hospital staff. Each day as I exited the elevator and made my way to Joe's room, it seemed like there was a chill in the air. There were no greetings or pleasantries exchanged as I walked past the nurses and aides.

Although the doctors felt they had the pneumonia under control, Joe had lost so much strength that he was unable to get out of bed or sit up without help. For someone with so much pride, this devastated him to such a degree that he spiraled downward into a depression and despondency that had us all greatly concerned. It seemed like this strong, positive, sharp-witted man had finally met his match, and the attitude of the nursing staff on this floor contributed to the problem.

When I walked into Joe's room each day, his lunch tray would still be in front of him, untouched. No one bothered to check if he had eaten. I was there for five hours or more daily, and no one came into the room to check on him unless I requested help. He seemed to have gone from having celebrity status to being just another ordinary patient. He demanded no attention, so he was given none. When dinner arrived I would cajole him to eat, encouraging him to pick up the fork or spoon. It would have been so much easier for me to hold his hand, cry with him, and feed him myself, but I knew I couldn't do that. It wouldn't help. I had to learn to be tough. I had to get him mad, and I had to get him motivated. At this point, our goal was to get him stronger so he could be transferred to the Rehab Center at Columbia, where he would receive three hours of physical therapy a day, but he wouldn't be accepted into the program until he grew stronger.

Our lowest point came when Joe refused PT with Dave. No matter how bad Joe felt, he always responded to Dave. The doctors got involved and began reading him the riot act. They told Joe they had done everything medically possible for him—now it was up to him and him alone. When they all left and we were by ourselves, he looked at me with such sadness in his eyes. I had seen plenty of anger in Joe's eyes over the years—a patient man he was not—and I had also seen plenty of love in those eyes toward me and our family and sorrow after the death of his brother, but this was a defeated look. I didn't know what to say. He spoke first, in a quiet, contemplative sort of way. "I've done everything they've asked of me without question. Today I just feel too tired to do PT with Dave, and they reprimand me. Doesn't everything else I've done count?"

My heart broke in two. I wanted to reach out to hold him and tell him, "Yes, everything else did count and it's okay," but I didn't. I couldn't. If I had, I would have sobbed and cried and screamed, "Why is this happening to us?"

That wouldn't have helped either one of us, especially Joe. I was walking out of that hospital, and I was going home. Joe was stuck there, alone, and the last thing he needed was an image of me being hysterical. I needed to be strong so he could be strong. I looked at him and prayed he saw the love in my eyes and simply said, "Tomorrow's a new day, Joe. Tomorrow will be better."

But things did not get better. The indifference of the staff astounded me. From the time we had first entered this hospital back in May, we came across nothing but wonderful, dedicated people. This floor was a whole new world.

All of this happening weeks before Christmas contributed to everyone's depression. There is nothing worse than being in New York City during the holiday season, surrounded by all the lights, music, and fanfare while you're on your way to visit a loved one in the hospital. On my trips every day I watched revelers coming from parties laughing, shoppers scurrying around balancing packages, Santa on every corner ringing his bell. I wanted the world to stop. How could everyone be so happy when I was so sad?

By this time, we knew Joe would not be home for the holiday. Now the goal needed to be redirected. I had to reassure Joe constantly that although he wouldn't be home this Christmas, we would be together for many Christmases to come. He just needed to get stronger.

The situation on the fifth floor got progressively worse. One day, Joe requested a bedpan, and it took forever for the patient aide to get one. She never came back to check on Joe even though we rang the bell several times. I went out in the hall looking for her, but no one was around either at the nurses' station or on the floor. Finally, I saw the aide come around a corner pushing a bed and called to her. I was told, rather sharply, that she needed to get this bed down to another floor and Joe would have to wait. I was dumbfounded.

I noticed Dr. Farr sitting at the nurse's station, so I approached her and explained the situation. She looked at me with shock on her face. Try as she may, she couldn't find a nurse, either. Finally, we saw the aide reappear. Dr. Farr requested that she go immediately to help Joe.

The aide retorted, "I'm going now!"

I observed this young woman get prepared. She walked slowly to the cart that held the supplies; there was no urgency in her steps. I watched as she picked up a pad, wipes, and rubber gloves. She purposely put on one pair of gloves and then methodically opened another package and put on another pair. I'm not a violent woman, but if I could have thrown her against a wall and strangled her, I would have. Where was her compassion, her caring?

Joe was now calling me every night at around midnight or one in the morning. He was begging me to get him transferred off the floor. "They don't care about me here. No one comes when I call or checks to see if I need anything," he told me. "Please, please, Jane—you have to get me transferred."

Although I had witnessed the incident with the aide, I still believed the nurses cared. How could they not? Was Joe so used to getting a lot of attention that he was missing his celebrity status? All these questions bounced around in my head. I kept reassuring him that, of course, everyone cared. I would tell him, "I'll see you in the morning. Try to get some sleep."

On another day Joe's central line started to seep blood. Because of his condition and the antibiotics he was taking, a central line had been inserted in Joe's neck, which was not a comfortable procedure, but it was a quicker way of getting the drugs into him and having blood drawn as often as he needed to. Central lines are necessary but can cause other issues. As Joe had this done several times, he was well aware of the implications of blood appearing on the bandage, so watching it seep through alarmed both of us. Was there a perforation of the vein? Was there a clot or an infection? These thoughts had to be swirling around in Joe's mind because the fear on his face was something I had never seen before. I called for a nurse. A very young nurse came into the room, took one look at Joe, and went into a panic, probably asking herself the same questions. She floundered, totally unable to assess the situation, and at this point Joe was terror-stricken. He kept screaming at me and the nurse to get a doctor. I think he thought he was going to bleed out or have a stroke. Panic kept building up inside me as I kept insisting to the nurse, "Get a doctor! Get a doctor now!" She kept telling me she could handle it, but it was very clear that she couldn't. "Get me a doctor now, or I'll get one myself!" I finally yelled at her.

She left the room and a few minutes later re-entered with a man. He walked by me, never identifying himself. I asked him, "Who are you? Where's the doctor?"

"I'm a PA; I can handle this."

"I want a doctor in here."

"There's no one available. I can handle this."

He started yelling out instructions to the nurse. Anything he asked for, she couldn't find. He finally screamed at her, "Then bring me some chucks, *now!*" He wrapped Joe's neck up with these large pads, trying to stop the bleeding. It took a while before finally everything was taken care of. My heart was pounding out of my chest. When it was time for me to go home, I couldn't imagine the loneliness Joe felt as I walked out of the room. I knew then that I had to get him transferred off that floor.

Things got even worse. We were hit with a big snowstorm, and there was no way I could get to the hospital. I called Joe during the day because I knew he needed to hear my voice, and I was upset that I couldn't be with him. As evening came, I tried to call again. He didn't answer. I hoped he was sleeping, but because of the situation on the floor, I started to get nervous. I called the nurse's station several times. No one answered, so I started to count the rings. The phone rang one hundred times before I hung up.

I was beside myself and called Lauren. "I can't get through to Dad. No one's answering at the station."

"Ok, Mom, I'll try him." After a while, Lauren called back.

"Mom, no one is answering. I counted the rings, too—120 times."

I can't explain the feeling of desperation I felt that night. The wind was howling outside, the snow was swirling around, and I was alone, not knowing what was happening to my husband. Finally, after several hours, I got in touch with him. I was so relieved to hear his voice, but he just kept telling me that no one cared, that no one was helping him. I heard someone talking in the background. "Joe, is there a nurse in the room?"

"Yes."

"Ok, please hand her the phone."

When she got on the phone, I realized it was a nurse I had a conversation with just a few days prior. She was the only nurse who came in when I was visiting. She showed me how to pound Joe's back to help keep his lungs clear. I had never seen anyone do this before. Because he was fighting pneumonia and now was unable to move around by himself, this was an important function. Why hadn't anyone shown me this while I sat with Joe five hours every day? When I met her, I felt so grateful that I finally had found someone who seemed to care.

She proved me wrong the night of the storm. When she got on the phone, she was distracted and not very friendly. It seemed like I was inconveniencing her. She told me Joe was "confused" and that she had to clean him up before her shift was over, which was shortly. She had no time to talk to me but I knew one thing for certain: Joe was never confused. In all he had gone through during these many months, Joe was never, ever confused. Every doctor we came in contact with was confident in having conversations with Joe about anything that was happening. The next day, I got to the hospital as soon as I could.

That was the last straw. I put in a request to the cardiologist who was now on rotation for a floor transfer for Joe. She had taken the biopsy after the second transplant on our first follow-up visit to Columbia. We liked her; she was pleasant and kind. Unfortunately, she didn't agree with me. "Mrs. Bavoso, this is a very competent cardiac care floor. Mr. Bavoso is getting quality care here. He's been through a lot, and maybe he feels like he's not getting the attention he was given before. I'll talk to him."

And she did, only managing to make things worse. Instead of reassuring Joe, she chastised him for calling me late at night, instructing him to just concentrate on getting stronger with Dave's help.

Again, he looked devastated. If there was anything I knew about my husband, it was that he didn't look for attention or want help from anyone if he could manage things himself. There was something terribly wrong with this floor. I was refused a transfer twice.

On December 22, just ten days after being sent to the fifth floor, Joe was back in the ICU and put on a ventilator. The pneumonia was back.

It's hard to remember how we all got through that Christmas. We had six children waiting for Santa Claus. Christmas was moved from my house to Lauren's. Peter, Janine, and the children stopped at Columbia on their way from New Jersey to Long Island.

The thought of Joe being alone on Christmas tore me apart. I had been with him the day before. His being back on a ventilator almost broke me. We had no conversation; I simply held his hand and reassured him we would get through this. There was no "he"; it was always "we." We were in this together like we had been in everything we had done for the past forty years.

Peter sat by his father's bedside. Janine and the kids waited in the car. Peter kept calling me, giving me updates. Joe was stable, but what was going through his mind was anyone's guess. With all he had been through to be back where he started on Christmas Day was more than anyone should have to bear. Peter was there for hours; I don't think he could pull himself away from his dad. The children were watching movies in the car. Certainly not a place for a five and seven-year-old to be spending Christmas. Finally, Peter had to say goodbye to Joe and leave. I think it was probably the hardest thing, up to that point, that he had ever done.

CHAPTER TWENTY-ONE

FEELING SAFE AGAIN

On the first full day that Joe was back in the ICU, I walked into the room while a nurse was moving him from side to side in the bed. She told me, "Your husband has small red spots on his body. That's the beginning of bedsores."

"Well, he wasn't taken very good care of on the fifth floor," I answered.

"What are you talking about? This man can't move on his own; he needs to be rotated every hour or he'll get bedsores."

"Unfortunately, no one did that in the other unit," I replied. The nurse just stared at me blankly.

"Well, don't worry. That won't happen here. Here he'll be moved every hour on the hour." I thanked her. I knew he was back in good hands.

Joe's being back in the ICU was devastating to all of us, but in a strange way it also brought me some peace. I knew that he was again being taken care of by caring, dedicated nurses. As I walked out of the hospital each evening, although the sorrow I felt was almost unbearable, I left without fear of his being neglected.

We had asked for, and were granted, a meeting with the cardiologist on rotation at the time, plus the nurse manager for the fifth floor and, of course, Dr. Mancini. The harm was done, but we knew that someone should be held accountable for what had happened. I typed up all the incidents that had occurred over the past ten days; I was ready with facts, dates, and times. Peter had done his own notetaking. He arrived at the hospital with his laptop and proceeded to take my place as the chief interrogator. I was glad to hand over the reins.

Dr. Mancini asked some questions of her own to the nurse manager, who offered no answers, only excuses. I had never seen this woman in the ten days I had spent on that floor. She seemed to have no clue as to what was going on in her unit. Dr. Mancini took her own notes, her eyes boring into the now very nervous nurse manager. At the end of the meeting, Peter looked directly at this nurse we had never met before and said, "When my father gets out of the ICU, we'll never allow him to be put back on the fifth floor. *Ever!*"

Dr. Mancini looked at the three of us. "Don't worry. I will *never* allow him to be put back in that unit."

As we walked outside of the conference room, the cardiologist approached me. "Mrs. Bavoso, I want to apologize. I should have listened to you. This is a lesson for me. I need to listen to the family". I looked at her and quietly said, "The one thing you have to remember is this. You do your rounds every day. You walk into a patient's room, read his chart, check his vitals, and leave. It takes no more than ten minutes. The family, especially my family, is here every day. We saw what was happening. Yes, you need to listen to the family." I felt no anger toward this doctor. I was too tired to be angry. I needed to save my energy for more positive things, but I did see the pain in her eyes.

The New Year was approaching, and I hoped 2010 would be a turn-around for us. Unfortunately, it wasn't meant to be. On New Year's Day, I got a call from Dr. Mancini. Joe had suffered a seizure at 9:30 a.m. Again, the three of us rushed to the hospital. He was sedated when we got there and had been sent for an MRI, which gave no indication of a stroke. A neurological angiogram was scheduled the next morning for 8 a.m.

Dr. Mancini walked into the room. I remember thinking, *Does this woman ever take a day off?* She looked at me with a concerned scowl. "Mrs. Bavoso, we have to see if Joe's responsive. Because if he isn't..."

Her voice trailed off. I knew what she was telling me. This could be it. I held my breath. She took her knuckles and rubbed them hard and fast along Joe's sternum, calling out his name over and over again. He opened his eyes. "Joe, do you know where you are? Blink once for yes and twice for no."

He blinked once.

"Okay. I'm going to ask you some questions. Answer them by blinking."

He answered each question correctly.

"He's back," she said. "We'll continue treatment. He'll have an evaluation tomorrow."

And she left the room as quietly as she entered it.

I knew Joe wasn't ready to give up; I knew in my heart that he was still fighting. After all, he was still my hero, the tough guy from Brooklyn.

We all got home around 10 p.m., including Joe's sister, who had decided to visit Joe on New Year's Day. I thought of how difficult and lonely it had been for her to drive the two hours back to New Jersey after witnessing all that had occurred. Joe was her big brother, though they were only eighteen months apart in age.

The next morning, Lauren and I arrived back at the hospital at 7:45 a.m. in time to see Joe before the scheduled neurological angiogram, a test that looks for a narrowing or blockage of a blood vessel or bleeding in the brain. We never wanted him to feel alone. He needed to see our faces, but we also needed to see his. The angiogram came back negative. At this point, Joe's platelet count was very low, and because of that, spontaneous bleeding can occur, which is what the doctors thought had happened. They put him on anti-seizure medication. He was already receiving platelets, but one of the antibiotics he was on lowered platelet counts. However, he couldn't come off of that medication because of the infection. It was a classic catch-22. The doctors ceased all sedation to evaluate his mental status. Most people on a ventilator are sedated because of the irritation of the tube down the throat. He was being challenged at every turn.

He had been on the vent for two weeks when I was again approached by Dr. Mancini. She said, "Mrs. Bavoso, Joe has been on the ventilator for fourteen days. Unfortunately, he still isn't strong enough to breath on his own. We need to do a tracheotomy to prevent another infection."

I was horrified, hardly able to catch my breath. A tracheotomy! She went on. "Mrs. Bavoso. This is reversible. It will make Joe much more comfortable, and it will prevent more infections. We'll schedule the procedure."

The tracheotomy was performed on January 6. Afterward, I braced myself and asked Joe the best I could, "Do you feel better without the tube down your throat?"

He nodded. He was also now on what we hoped would be temporary dialysis. His kidneys were taking a hit with the infections and the drop in blood pressure.

Dave came by and had him move his fingers, toes, hands, and feet. Dave told Joe they had a lot of work to do. Joe nodded. Jenn stopped by for a visit. Every doctor and nurse I spoke with kept telling me that Joe was "one tough guy." I learned that a long time ago.

I reminded Joe every chance I had that everyone was pulling and praying for him and that the children were waiting for him to come home. They kept asking, "When is Papa coming home? We haven't seen him for such a long time." It broke our hearts. We were all so tired and weary, but then we would think, "How tired and weary is Joe?" We were trying our best to keep him positive, to tell him he could do this—again. I felt like a commuter with no paying job at the end of my daily trip. But my job was to be there every day. I needed for him to see me, I needed to encourage him and tell him he was going to make it.

I was still sending out my updates. The list of recipients was getting longer. People were sharing my emails with others. I ended my email on January 6 with this paragraph:

This was a long update, but so much has happened in the past weeks. I really don't even remember anymore what day it is, much less what the date is. One day just becomes the next. I am not going to ask you to pray for Joe because I know you all are. I sincerely thank you for that. Since October 1, Joe has only been home for five days—I miss him. I miss eating breakfast with him and sharing the newspaper. I miss sitting on the couch and watching a movie together. I miss coming home from work and him saying, "Don't cook—let's go out tonight." I miss following him around carrying his camera equipment so he can get the best sunset shot. I miss his sense of humor. I need him home. We have lots of things to do. I think I will end this update the way Joe signed off on all of his political commentaries:

THANKS FOR LISTENING.

CHAPTER TWENTY-TWO

Hanging On

The following week, we started to see some progress. Joe finished all the antibiotics for the pneumonia and his kidneys started to function well on their own. All the central lines in Joe's neck and groin were removed. The doctors were trying to wean him off the ventilator a little each day to strengthen his lungs. His color was looking good, and the best news of all was that his sixth biopsy came back negative—no rejection! Everyone held their breath when a biopsy was performed. Having taken Joe off the anti-rejection drugs always left him in jeopardy.

Unfortunately, his platelet count was still low, and the hematology team was trying to figure out why. Because the low count is what caused the seizure, he was kept on anti-seizure medication.

Dave was back, working with Joe to help him once again gain strength. I observed as Dave encouraged Joe with every effort he made. I watched this husband of mine, and my heart broke at the utter weakness of his body. I saw him struggle to lift his arm and hold it up for fifteen seconds and then as he tried to push his feet against Dave's hand. There was no way he could lift his legs. Those once-powerful legs I always admired were now devoid of muscle mass. Both Dave and I cheered him on, but the pain on Joe's face made me want to yell out, "*Please stop!*" But I couldn't. The only way Joe was going to get home was to build up his muscles, and that was going to cause pain.

I joked with Dave, "Wait until Joe's off the vent; he'll have lots to say to you."

Dave's answer was always the same. "He can say whatever he wants to me when he's walking out the door of this hospital and we're going for a beer together."

Dave would look at Joe and say over and over again, "If you can move it, Joe, I can make it stronger."

As Joe slept, I gazed out the window and noticed ice floating in the Hudson River.

It dawned on me that I had watched each season pass through the windows of the New York Columbia-Presbyterian Hospital. The view was beautiful, each period bringing its own special something to be admired. I had watched the sunrise and set; the blue skies of a warm summer morning; and the gray, cold skies of a frigid winter afternoon, but I was tiring of Columbia and glancing at the Hudson River. I was worn out from all the heartbreak in the ICU.

I was drained watching the Chinese mother who spoke little English caring for her daughter every day, her seriously ill daughter who had been in the ICU for months. One day, I asked this woman how her daughter was doing. She seemed to understand me and moved her hand to indicate, "So-so." I told her I would keep her daughter in my thoughts and prayers. She nodded her head with a silent thank you. Her eyes looked so sad and vacant, and I thought of how isolated this woman must have felt each day. I was able to chat with the nurses; she couldn't converse with them, but each day she was there, keeping a vigil for her child.

The woman two rooms down from Joe passed away. I saw her husband each day, walking the halls. I watched the doctor give him a hug and promise him they would make his wife as comfortable as possible. And then I saw their grandchildren come to say their goodbyes.

There were wonderful success stories at Columbia, but at the time I was only aware of the sad ones, and I wanted to leave them behind.

Yes, I was sick of Columbia, but I knew I would be there for some time to come because Joe still had a long way to go.

* * *

Being at the hospital for most of the day, I was ushered in and out of Joe's room quite often. I disliked going into the family lounge—it was always too loud and crowded for me—and I only went to the cafeteria to grab a cup of tea when Joe was sleeping. I would never let him see me sipping a drink. Because Joe was on a ventilator, he hadn't had any liquids in his mouth for weeks. At times, when he was sleeping, I would see him licking his lips or sticking his tongue out as though he were licking an ice cream cone. I was positive he was dreaming about ice cream because that was one of Joe's dietary downfalls, along with any kind of cookie. If we were out walking on the East End, Joe couldn't resist stopping for ice cream. He could never understand my refusal to join him. "You don't want any ice cream?" he would say to me, almost in disgust. "Nope, I'm good" was usually my answer, and then he would proceed to walk inside, shaking his head in disbelief while he purchased his double-scoop cone. So I was pretty sure his dreams were of something cool and cold and soothing going down his throat, and it was always painful for me to watch, knowing how parched he was.

I soon discovered my "safe space": a window with a large sill at the end of the hall afforded me the solitude I needed. I would often sit there and look out the panes of glass, watching the activity on the city street below. Cars, buses, and taxis speeding by, people walking in every direction, each person rushing to get to their destination. Here I could also keep an eye on Joe's room and notice when the curtain was pulled back from the big glass walls, when whatever procedure or testing was being done was finally over. I would then return and take my seat once more next to the bed.

It's funny how you almost become possessive of something just because you use it often. If I approached my window and someone else was sitting there, I was almost outraged. How dare someone else be sitting in my space!

But there I met the son of the Chinese lady and the family of another heart transplant patient who was also back in the hospital because of an infection.

I was so thankful I could be with Joe every day. I absolutely knew it helped him keep his sanity. Although we couldn't converse, I would update him on what was happening in our family. We talked—or rather, I talked— about everything under the sun. I wanted to keep him informed and in tune with the world as best I could. The nurses all chatted with Joe because they always got some sort of response from him, either a big smile or a frown or the rolling of his eyes. He connected with them and they with him.

His window curtain was pulled open each morning. It was important for him to distinguish between night and day and between one day and the next. Someone in a hospital bed for as long as Joe loses track of time. Amazingly, Joe was trying to keep track of time on his own. He was a man of determination and kept track of not only his days but of the date. I would ask him a question, and he would mouth the answer. I was getting pretty good at reading his lips, and at times he was able to write me a few words. At home, he always did the crossword puzzle in the newspaper each morning, so Lauren enlarged a few crosswords and brought them to the hospital. I would read him the clue, and before I had a chance to think about it, Joe was already trying to write the answer in the boxes. He was bent on keeping his mind as sharp as he could.

I know this is why the doctors and the nurses took such a special interest in him. Joe was a fighter and an inspiration to all who came in contact with him.

CHAPTER TWENTY-THREE

TRYING TO HOLD ON TIGHT

For a while, things seemed to be going well. A respiratory therapist was now working with Joe. It was essential to wean him off the vent to enable him to be released from the ICU. Each time I walked into Joe's room and saw him on the CPAP (continuous positive airway pressure therapy) machine I would encourage him: "You can do it, Joe; please, just a little longer." The more time he could tolerate off the vent, the more hope I had that he was going to beat this and walk out of the hospital. I didn't care if it was in three weeks or three months, I just wanted him to come home. When he would shake his head indicating to me that he was finished for the day, a feeling of disappointment came crashing down on me. I don't know if he saw it in my eyes; I hope he never did. There was nothing in the past nine months that Joe had done that had disappointed me. I knew it wasn't fair to put so much pressure on him, but I was desperate to get our life back.

Joe also had a feeding tube, which was threaded through his nose and down his throat, and I knew it was very irritating. Every once in a while, he would try to adjust it to a more comfortable position, and I cringed each time he attempted it. He was so weak, and it took so much effort to lift his hand to his face only to move the tube a fraction of an inch. At one point, the doctors decided to remove the tube from his nose and place it directly into his stomach. I should have been as horrified at that as I was when he got the trach, but I wasn't. I was told this was also reversible and would help Joe be more comfortable.

I knew Joe was going to be here for the long haul, so I was always on board for anything that would make him feel better. But I also thought how nice it would be to look at Joe's face without that yellow tube. It would be hidden under the blanket, and I could pretend it didn't exist. However, a sonogram of the abdomen was performed, and it determined there was still too much fluid in the area to safely insert the tube. Joe couldn't catch a break.

His kidneys had taken some big hits with the infections. He wasn't urinating as much as he should, but the doctors were trying to avoid catheterization. When Joe would indicate to me that he needed the urinal, I was almost ecstatic. It was like getting excited about your toddler asking to use the potty. After he was finished, I would note the ccs and save it for the nurse. Every drop had to be recorded. He had already been on temporary dialysis a few times, so every little normal function of the kidneys was celebrated. Unfortunately, even that decision was reversed, and eventually, a catheter was inserted.

Each day when I walked off the elevator and entered the ICU, I never knew what I was going to find, so I prayed all the way to the hospital, *Please God, just let today go well. Please don't let anything bad happen today.*

No one seemed to be listening. When I arrived at the hospital on February 24, I found Peter and Joe's brother John surrounded by a group of doctors. Joe had gone into atrial fibrillation and spiked a fever. His blood pressure had dropped dangerously low, and all the central lines that had just been taken out a few weeks before were now put back in. It was determined that he had another urinary tract infection, just after having one-two weeks prior. The doctors removed the catheter, thinking that maybe it was the cause of the infections. It was becoming a guessing game. We left the hospital at 2:30 a.m.

After each previous episode, Joe's kidneys had managed to bounce back, but this time the doctors were giving us slim hope that it would happen again. Joe was set up for dialysis three times a week. This setback hit me like a punch to my gut. I felt like I was being pummeled every day by an opponent who was bigger and stronger and out of my league.

Yet I never had any doubts about Joe. After about two weeks he started to rally, and for the next three weeks, I watched him gaining strength. Dave would look over at me and say excitedly, "Did you see that? He's getting stronger every day!" He was now able to get Joe in an upright position, sitting on the side of the bed, while I supported him from behind. Dave always amazed me.

Joe was not ready to give up. He had too much to come home to. He was fighting tooth and nail, and even the most hardened, war-weary doctors were in awe. He was progressing so well that one day Dr. Farr while walking by, stopped and called out to Dave. "Hey Dave, when you get Joe up and walking, I'll buy you a bottle of champagne."

"You're on!" Dave exclaimed good-naturedly. "But I want a really good bottle of champagne. No Korbel for me!"

Dave included Joe in the bet. "Joe, on the day you're discharged from the hospital, we're going to open that bottle of champagne and have a glass together."

I teased Dave, asking if that would be allowed. "On that day," he said, "it will definitely be allowed!"

We had now been at Columbia so long that everyone in the ICU knew us. I would meet people in the halls or on my way to grab a cup of tea in the cafeteria, and I would be stopped and asked how Joe was doing or told they heard my husband was doing really well. Many times I would have to ask myself where or when I met the person; I was losing track of all the people who had crossed our paths these many months, but they always remembered us. Anyone who passed Joe's room would catch my eye and give me a thumbs up. I was feeling positive vibes all around me.

March 21, Joe's birthday, was quickly approaching. We were almost wishing he wouldn't remember. Joe was the guy who taught me the fun of celebrating birthdays. My family never celebrated those milestones.

When I started dating Joe at just shy of fifteen years old, he was almost incredulous that birthdays weren't all that important to me. "Your birthday is the only day in the year that's your own," he lectured me. And from that day forward, he taught me how to celebrate a birthday. He never forgot my birthday or anyone else's who he called a friend. For all the years of our marriage, I woke up on my birthday with a big handmade Happy Birthday sign hung on the wall. A card would be waiting on the kitchen table, always with a note written inside. Roses would be delivered to my office, and dinner reservations would be made. Surprise trips were planned for those special birthdays. Joe was the king of birthdays! So now we were faced with a dilemma. How were we going to make this one special for him? Joe needed—and we needed—to celebrate that he was still with us, fighting every day to come home.

Lauren came up with the plan. She decided she would bring our youngest grandchild, 18-month-old Hannah, to the hospital to visit Papa. She was the logical choice: too young to really understand, yet old enough to flirt and show off for her grandfather.

I received permission from the nurses. When Hannah arrived in her stroller with a big "Happy Birthday" balloon attached, I asked the nurse to turn Joe toward the door. I told him we had a birthday surprise for him. I held my breath waiting for his reaction. His face was beaming with a big smile!

Hannah called out his name and waved. She recited her vocabulary for him and charmed all the nurses. Joe hadn't seen any of the children for six months. He always referred to Hannah as our "miracle baby," the one who never was supposed to be here. The one he held so tightly and rocked in his arms when she was an infant. The visit lasted for about thirty minutes, but I know if Joe could have said anything, he would have told me it was the best birthday gift he ever received.

Joe continued to progress and was able to tolerate more and more time off the vent. We were starting to see a light at the end of the tunnel.

CHAPTER TWENTY-FOUR

FALLING BACK IN THE PIT

Eight days later, when I walked into Joe's room, I made a mental note to myself about how good he looked. He was still very weak, but his eyes were bright and clear, and he was managing to write me notes more easily. He told me he had a great workout with Dave that morning, and later in the afternoon, Dave confirmed that.

Joe couldn't roll over or sit up in the bed by himself. Besides the nurses turning him every hour, an orderly had to rotate Joe's body to change the sheets and the pads on the bed. We got to know most of them, but our favorite was Marcus, a tall African American man with dreadlocks like Bob Marley. He always entered the room with his big smile and big personality. He greeted Joe like a good friend and Joe reciprocated with a broad smile and thumbs up. Marcus and I always chatted and, on some days, when the hospital was short-staffed, I would help Marcus move Joe.

The first time I offered, he asked me, "Are you sure you can do this? Joe's dead weight, you know."

"I've been here for quite a few months, and I've watched this procedure over and over again. I can do this with you."

"Okay, then. Let's get started." And we did.

He never questioned me again. Joe also knew the drill. He would fold his arms across his chest and get ready to be rolled. I often thought of how humiliating this whole procedure was to a man who was always so proud of being independent and doing everything on his own. "Jane, you're not my mother," was his standard answer to me when I offered to mother him over the years during some episodes with a virus or flu. And here he was, totally dependent on others.

When I arrived the next day and walked into Joe's room, I noticed that his BP was extremely low and his heart rate was accelerated. The first thing we all had learned to do when we entered Joe's room was to check his numbers. I observed my children on many days—without even realizing it, they all looked immediately up to the monitors. On this day, Joe's numbers weren't good. I alerted the nurse, and everything started all over again. Joe was spiking a fever, and his blood pressure had dropped. All central lines, which had just been removed, were once again put back in. Cultures were taken, medications were administered.

I arrived home that night at 10:00 p.m. When I entered my house, I hung up my coat and walked into the bedroom, exhausted. And then - finally - it hit me. I started to cry; not just cry, but sob and wail. I couldn't control myself. I screamed at God. It was the first time during this entire ordeal that I yelled at the Almighty. I pounded on the walls and screamed as loud as I could, demanding, "I want my husband back! Give me Joe back! What else do You want from us? We've done everything to keep our faith. We trusted in You! We can't give You anymore, there's nothing left to give. He's a good man; he just wants to come home to his family. Please, please have mercy on us."

I knew the windows were all closed and that no one could hear me. It's funny, during one of my darkest moments, I was still worried about what the neighbors would think.

The outburst lasted just a few minutes before I fell on the bed, totally exhausted and spent, sobbing into the pillows until eventually sleep overtook me. The next day I got up, rode the train, and arrived at the hospital at my usual time.

Amazingly, by Friday, Joe was looking and feeling better. The medical team could not find the source of the infection, although because of the fever they assured me he had one. The cultures came back negative. They saw some bleeding and ordered a CT scan, but that also came back negative. This top-rate medical team at one of the most prestigious hospitals in the country all stood around scratching their heads.

Dave came back almost immediately and started PT all over again. The hardest part for me, and most certainly for Joe, was that with each incident he would lose all the progress he had gained working with Dave. He was starting from square one over and over again, and yet he never refused Dave. Every doctor I spoke with after every setback would reassure me that Joe could get better. They saw his determination and outlook and knew that he was a fighter and would never give up.

I felt like we were in the bottom of a pit trying to claw our way to the top, and when we almost got there, we would lose our grip and fall back down again.

After this incident, Joe told me he never thought it would be this hard. I bent over closer to him and looked him straight in the eyes. "Neither did I, but you're still here, and we're going to keep fighting and climbing until we reach our goal."

He nodded his head in agreement. My job was to keep hope alive, and I wasn't anywhere near ready to give up on that.

Another time, he asked me what day it was, and when I told him it was Tuesday, he seemed upset. I asked why, and he explained to me that he was trying to keep track of the days of the week as a mental exercise, and he thought it was Wednesday.

"Seriously, Joe? That's why you're upset? Don't beat yourself up over that; many times, even when things were normal, I forgot what day of the week it was. Cut yourself some slack."

But Joe never cut himself any slack. He wanted to get better physically, and he knew how important it was to keep his mind sharp, too. I knew this was why the doctors took such an interest in him and were cheering him on. After all he had been through, he never threw in the towel. He was pretty extraordinary, even at Columbia.

I continued to bring to the hospital every birthday, get well, and Mass card Joe received. Every day, my mailbox was filled with cards for Joe. It was so important for him to know that he wasn't forgotten because the walls of this hospital room had to be closing in on him. Joe wasn't a couch potato; he was an active guy who had many plans for life.

Because he was keenly aware of days and dates, he knew Easter would be upon us soon. This is the time of the year when Joe would be buying flowers to plant in his garden. I was never a gardener, but he loved it. He would make a trip to the nursery himself and bring back a variety of flowers to plant. He would educate me on what each one was, how tall they would get, which would bloom first, and which needed sun or shade. I would listen intently and then leave him to his task. He was always happy planting in the dirt. I was always happy with the outcome. It was a win-win situation for us both. I was positive he was thinking about his garden and probably worrying about it too since it was now left to me. He also knew Easter would be here, another holiday for him to miss. Although he didn't mention it, I'm sure he was thinking about the Easter egg hunt, the baskets, the coloring of eggs.

I felt a heaviness in my chest, and the only way I could explain the feeling was that my heart felt as if it were broken in two. There was no way that I could patch it or sew it or fix it. I knew it was going to remain this way until I could get Joe out of the hospital. I braced myself, knowing this feeling would be with me for some time to come.

CHAPTER TWENTY-FIVE

ANOTHER MISSED HOLIDAY

Easter Sunday found me driving to the hospital instead of taking my usual train ride. I thought that if I drove I would get home faster because, honestly, I didn't want to go to the hospital that morning.

But I would never leave Joe alone on any day, let alone a holiday. If for any reason I couldn't get to the hospital, I would arrange for someone else to take my place. I always wanted him to have a family member or a friend to keep him company, at least for a few hours each day.

But on this holiday I just wanted to stay home. Lauren was hosting dinner. Peter, Janine, and the kids were coming, and I had made all the children their baskets. I longed for a somewhat normal holiday, although I knew in my heart it really couldn't be.

I attended church in the morning, picked up a box of chocolates for the nurses, and, with a heavy heart, started my drive. The hospital was very quiet that day, as it usually is on a holiday. I stopped by the nurses' station, greeted them with a "Happy Easter," and dropped off the chocolates. When I entered Joe's room, he was awake and gazing out the window. The curtains were pulled back, and the sun was shining in. It was an early Easter, but the sun was strong that day, and although it was a little chilly, the promise of spring was in the air.

He smiled at me, and I sat by his side. I have no recollection of what I spoke to him about. He knew of the activities that were happening at home. We had always hosted Easter, and since the grandchildren had been born it became even more exciting and fun. Six grandchildren born in six years gave us lots of craziness during recent holidays. As each child arrived, just as I had a Christmas stocking made with their name on it to hang in our house, I also ordered a personalized Easter basket for each of them. Joe would be shooting photos from the start of the day until the end, although getting a group shot always eluded him. He would laugh and say, "It's like herding cats," one of his favorite expressions regarding the kids. He was right—it was tough to get six little ones to sit still long enough for a group photo.

I knew all those thoughts were going through his head. I was at a loss for words; what could I possibly talk about? He had been in this hospital since November, and now it was spring. And, God forgive me, all I kept thinking about was going home. I don't know if I was getting to a breaking point or had anxiety that day, but I just wanted to run out of that hospital as quickly as I could. I sat with Joe for a few hours, not my usual all-day routine, watching the clock. Finally, I kissed him goodbye and said, "I'll see you tomorrow." Joe looked at me and nodded. I can't imagine how he felt, knowing the rest of us would all be together.

Traffic was light, and I made it home in time for the children's Easter egg hunt and dinner. I didn't enjoy either one; Joe's presence was always missed. The three oldest were constantly asking, "When is Papa coming home? He's been gone so long." I would always reassure them with the same response. "Papa's trying so hard to get better. He misses you every day."

Each night at dinner, the kids would say grace and end their prayer with "Go, Joe." It had become our ritual. So although I wanted so badly to be present at home, my thoughts were with Joe in that lonely hospital room. I couldn't tear myself away from reality no matter how hard I tried.

We said grace, raised our glasses, and shouted out in unison, "Go, Joe!" The next morning, I once again found myself on the LIRR and the subway headed to the hospital.

I knew I needed to be with Joe every day so he would never feel alone, and I also knew he needed me to be his vigilant advocate because he couldn't speak for himself. It must have been so frustrating to this man who was always in charge of everything.

One day, when Joe still had a catheter, he started to express to me that he was in pain. The pain was getting increasingly more intense, so I summoned the nurse. After a while, a resident walked into the room. At this point, Joe was almost in tears, which was unusual for him. This doctor in training took her time in assessing the situation and stood there guessing. I told her I wanted one of the urology fellows because it was clear to anyone that the problem was getting worse and the source of the pain had to be the catheter. She stood her ground, telling me she was capable of handling this. Meanwhile, nothing was happening except the situation was getting worse. She was a tall, very attractive young woman, very sure of herself and her position. However, her position meant nothing to me.

Interns are doctors too, but I wouldn't put my life in their hands. Experience plays a big part of any profession. Joe's facial expressions and his eye contact told me he wanted one of the urology fellows in that room. He needed help immediately. Residents rotated every four weeks to a different unit, so each month we would start with a new group. This young doctor told me how many weeks she had been on this floor and how knowledgeable she was. I found through my experience at Columbia that most of the residents were full of themselves. Who could blame them? They had a coveted residency at one of the best hospitals in the country. Certainly a remarkable accomplishment for any young doctor. At the moment, however, I was not impressed.

I looked her straight in the eye and took a deep breath. "Listen, lady, you may have been in this unit for a few weeks, but I've been here for six long months. I know every inch of this place and how it works. I'm telling you right now to get a urologist in here immediately, or I'll get one myself." My not addressing her as doctor shocked me as much as it did her, but I was angry and Joe couldn't speak for himself, so at that moment I was his voice. She got the urologist.

Another time, when Joe was again fighting an infection, he seemed really upset, and I knew he was frightened. How many times could he be thrown back to start all over again? How many times was he expected to be brave? He indicated to me that he wanted to see Dr. Mancini. As I've mentioned before, Dr. Mancini always made Joe feel better. He trusted her explicitly. I walked to the station and sitting there was a young resident. Rotations had started again, and he had no idea who I was or how long I had been there. I asked him quietly, "Would you please call Dr. Mancini for me? Tell her Joe Bavoso needs to see her."

He looked at me like I had two heads. "I can't call Dr. Mancini," he said almost indignantly.

I reassured him, "It's okay. My husband has been here for months. Dr. Mancini gave me her number to call whenever I felt I needed her." And that was the God's honest truth, but he decided to call what he thought was my bluff.

"Well, if you have her number, why don't you call her yourself?" he asked in a sarcastic tone.

"Okay, I will." I turned away from him and went back to Joe's room. Just as I took out my phone and started scrolling for Dr. Mancini's number, the infectious disease doctor came in. With all of Joe's infections, we had gotten to know Dr. Tsiouris very well.

"How's everything?" he asked in his usual friendly way.

"Joe seems a little upset today, and he asked to see Dr. Mancini. The doctor at the desk refused to call her for me, so I'm calling her myself. She gave me her number."

"The resident at the desk refused?" he asked, with a confused look on his face.

"Yes."

"Put your phone away. I'll handle this."

I watched as he walked directly towards the desk, had a quick conversation, and returned to Joe's room. "Dr. Mancini will be here shortly."

The young, full-of-himself doctor at the desk looked rather sheepish when he saw Dr. Mancini come down the hall not five minutes later. She entered the room and asked Joe what the problem was. She then asked Lauren and me to step outside for a minute.

We walked down the hall towards my safe-space window to wait. As we stood there, I noticed the young doctor at the desk trying to catch my eye. He looked at me with a big smile and a thumbs up. I glared back at him and turned my back.

I don't know what Dr. Mancini said to Joe, but he was calmer when we returned to the room, and the young doctor at the desk didn't try to catch my glance again.

And then there was the psychiatrist that wouldn't give Joe an antidepressant after the first heart failed. I rarely saw him; I didn't know if he even visited Joe. But one day while I was there, he showed up. "You know, Mrs. Bavoso, it's very difficult for me to talk to your husband. I can't understand what he's trying to say to me."

"Well, I'm here every day. Why don't you visit when I'm here? I've gotten pretty good at reading his lips. I could interpret for you."

"I do my rounds early in the morning," he said—and yet here he was at noon. "But how are you doing?" he inquired. This man was tall, around six foot two. He would stand with his arms bent at the elbow, hands entwined across his chest looking down on me. The question and his stance irritated me.

"I'm fine. Don't worry about me. You just worry about Joe," I answered rather brusquely.

I never saw him again, but I'm sure he stuck his head in the doorway on his morning rounds to nod at Joe. I hope he at least did that because I received plenty of bills from him.

And those were only three of the reasons I knew I had to be with Joe every day. He had no voice; I had now become his voice.

CHAPTER TWENTY-SIX

ANOTHER DETOUR IN THE JOURNEY

Joe was in very poor condition, but for the next few weeks everything remained stable, and Dave continued working with him. When Dave entered the room, Joe was all smiles; it had become the highlight of our day.

The biggest obstacle was trying to wean Joe off the vent. To test Joe's ability to speak, the respiratory therapist decided to adjust the trach, enabling air to move through Joe's vocal cords. She then encouraged Joe to say something. I watched as he attempted to formulate a sentence. This was his opportunity, and he didn't want to blow it. After a minute or two, the therapist, knowing he was struggling, suggested, "Joe, just say one word."

It took quite an effort, but the first word he chose to say was my name. It was the first time in over six months I had heard his voice. It was weak and quiet, not the strong, powerful voice I was used to, but it was Joe's voice, and I accepted it as a gift because, Jane, was the only word he managed to say.

Next, the decision was made to try the swallow test. If he were able to swallow a small amount of pureed food, the chances were good that the feeding tube could be removed eventually.

We all knew it was a long shot, but I watched, praying and hoping. Joe was given a spoonful of thickened liquid. Please, God, let him be able to do this, I silently pleaded. He tried, God knows he tried, but he couldn't get the liquid down his throat. I was devastated. I just wanted one more small ray of hope, something more to cling to after another long day.

Joe had dialysis three times a week. The procedure is awful for anyone, but for someone in Joe's condition, it was even worse. The huge machine was wheeled into his room, taking up much of the space. The technician stayed for the full four hours. It was a complicated machine, but after asking questions and observing it for weeks I was able to understand some of the gauges. It left Joe totally exhausted. No matter how many blankets we put on him, he was always shivering. I walked in and out of his room during the treatment. I needed to go to my safe space to take a deep breath, to pray a few silent prayers, and to gaze out the window at the world outside, if only for a few minutes.

One day during dialysis, the nephrologist who had been treating Joe's kidney issues stopped by. He was one of the top kidney doctors at Columbia, and we felt fortunate to have him caring for Joe. He was always pleasant and supportive, but that day his words shocked me.

"Mrs. Bavoso, I don't want you to worry about the kidneys." he said to me. "Our concern is to get your husband better and the infections under control. The heart is showing no sign of rejection, which is wonderful. Unfortunately, I don't believe the kidneys will ever totally come back, but when Joe is strong again, we can always do a kidney transplant."

I stood there, dumbfounded. *A kidney transplant!* He said it so casually, as if he were talking about a car. "Well, the engine is working great now, but the carburetor needs to be replaced. No big deal."

I had no response. I was speechless. I couldn't imagine going through this ordeal again with another organ. But I also knew that if necessary, Joe and I would both do this all over again. I would have done anything to save Joe's life, and he would have done anything to get his life back, but at that moment I couldn't respond.

Joe continued to hold his own and because of that Peter decided to bring Jack, our oldest grandchild, for a visit. "Are you sure you should take him?" I asked. "He's only seven; it might traumatize him too much."

"Mom, Jack keeps asking about Dad. He misses him. He's drawing pictures of him and dad on a boat fishing. I think it would do them both good. They haven't seen each other for almost seven months."

And so, on a Sunday, Jack visited his Papa. Knowing that Joe would not be alone, I stayed home that day to give myself a little respite. Peter included me in the visit by sending me pictures.

We now had started to gown up when we entered Joe's room. Outside was a cart with gowns and gloves we had to put on before we could enter. At first, I thought it was to protect Joe, but then I realized it was to protect the visitor. Joe had now developed a *Clostridioides difficle,* commonly called C. diff, a bacterium that can cause symptoms ranging from diarrhea to life-threatening inflammation of the colon. Just another thing Joe had to deal with. I felt like I was in a hazmat suit and Joe was some alien I dared not get close to. I hated visiting him that way, but we never talked about it; it just became part of our daily routine.

So there was Jack, this seven year old, gowned up and sitting next to his Papa's hospital bed, reading his storybook to his grandfather. Upon his return home, he told his mother, "I was so happy to see Papa. But you know what, Mommy, I think Papa was just as happy to see me." He was absolutely right.

And so it went for the next few weeks. I knew Joe had a tough battle ahead, but we never gave up hope. Hope was the only thing we had. If he could just hold his own, if the infections were controlled, if the heart kept functioning, if he could just gain some strength working with Dave, I knew that Joe would make it. There were so many ifs, but he wasn't ready to throw in the towel, and neither was I. He was fighting every day, and I was fighting alongside him.

On one of those quiet days, one of the cardiologists came by while Joe was sleeping. He pulled up a chair and sat next to me. He started the conversation with, "He's doing really well right now."

"He seems to be," I answered. "Let's just hope it continues."

"Yes, Mrs. Bavoso, but we have to think, where do we go from here? What can we do to make him stronger?"

I listened with interest while the doctor continued. "Try as we may, Columbia is not set up to wean someone from a ventilator who has been on it as long as Joe has. You need a special facility for that. The cardiac team has been discussing this, and we think you should consider transferring Joe, now that he seems more stable, to a special facility located in Wayne, New Jersey. They accept patients in Joe's condition, and they are specially trained to help get people off a vent. Joe needs to get off the vent to improve. We've done our best, but again, we're not equipped for that type of therapy."

My first thought was, "How am I going to get to Wayne, New Jersey, every day to be with Joe?" I couldn't imagine not seeing him on a daily basis. I would have to limit my visits to a few times a week, I told myself.

The doctor continued. "I'll give you some brochures to look over, and I can make arrangements to have a representative from the facility meet you and your family here to discuss the possibility of transfer."

I thanked the doctor and told him I would discuss it with my children, but I was sure we would agree to meet with the special facility rep. As much as I didn't want Joe to leave Columbia for another institution, I also knew we would do anything to get him back home.

And then, without warning, within the next hour, Joe's fever spiked to 102 degrees. Once again, we started our long climb out of the hole.

Lauren had stopped by the hospital after finishing teaching her class at F.I.T. in the city, and she watched with me as things went from bad to worse.

Joe seemed to go from fine to ill in a flash. Lauren and I wouldn't leave his side. Peter arrived at the hospital at around 10 p.m. This was the sickest we had seen Joe in all the months since he received the second heart.

At one point he was trying to mouth something to Peter. "What, Dad? What can I do for you?" After a few moments, Peter turned to me. "Mom, he's asking for a priest."

That's when I knew things were really bad. In all the months, Joe had been at Columbia, with all the ups and downs he had gone through, he had never asked for a priest. I went to the nurses' station and inquired if one was available. By this time it was close to midnight. Within ten minutes, a priest arrived.

He gave Joe absolution and blessed him, and we all recited the Our Father together, including the male nurse who was on the night shift. As weak as Joe was, he managed to make the Sign of the Cross. I looked at this fighter in the bed, this man who would never give up, and knew he was making his peace with God. I asked him if he felt better, and he nodded. This was the first time hope started to fade for me.

Cultures were taken, and they showed that Joe had two different types of bacteria in his blood and had once again developed pneumonia. Of course, central lines were put in, and antibiotics were administered immediately. Amazingly, Joe continued to hang on, astonishing every doctor at Columbia. He never gave us any indication he was giving up. He was a true warrior—one of a world of reasons I loved him so much.

CHAPTER TWENTY-SEVEN

THE DAYS ARE DWINDLING

After the last setback, Joe continued to hold his own, although he physically returned back to where he had started months ago. That was the most difficult thing for me to witness: the total weakness of his body after so much effort and hard work. The reality had set in.

Joe was never going to get out of Columbia. I had finally come to terms with it.

He had come back so many times only to be shot down again and again. This was the final act, the closing curtain. I took each day as a miracle, and Joe didn't disappoint me. On June 4 I walked into his room and inquired whether he knew what day it was. He mouthed to me, "Happy Birthday." With all he had gone through, with his body completely devoid of strength, racked with infection and fighting pneumonia, with what I knew—and I'm sure he knew—was only a few days or weeks left, this man, this lover of birthdays, remembered it was mine.

As I think back on that day, I realize that this was the most wonderful gift he had ever given me.

Peter was determined to get the kids back up to see their Papa. He took five-year-old Julia for a quick visit. She left Papa a beaded bracelet with the words *I Love You* spelled out.

Jack was getting anxious to visit Joe again, but this time the visit was different because his Papa was so much more ill. I was there during that visit, and the one thing I will have forever in my memory is Joe, with so much effort, reaching out his hand and taking Jack's face in it. He mouthed the words *I love you* to his firstborn grandson, and Jack, knowing exactly what his Papa had said, responded without hesitation, "I love you too, Papa."

On June 6, Lauren surprised Joe with a visit from the twins, who were turning three the following week. Joe had not seen them for seven months. A pulmonary doctor had just stepped out of Joe's room when the twins arrived. The look on this doctor's face was priceless when he saw these two toddlers coming down the hall. I told him they were our grandchildren and how long it had been since Joe had seen them.

I then saw the emotion in his eyes as they filled with tears. "Bring them in; this is exactly what he needs."

We gowned up those two babies and held them in our arms. I could never put into words the expression on Joe's face. He couldn't hug the children or kiss them, although Nora insisted that she wanted to "give Papa a kiss," and Luke told Papa he wanted to "get rid of all that stuff on you," but Joe's eyes beamed with so much love and gratitude when he saw his babies.

To this day, I am so grateful to my children that they insisted on taking the kids to the hospital. I know it helped Joe find some peace in his final days.

Each day, as I sat with Joe and watched him get weaker and weaker, the life slowly fading from his body, I kept thinking to myself, *How am I going to handle this?*

I had used up all my strength. How was I going to get through what I knew was coming?

All throughout this journey, the people I was close to advised me, "Just ask the doctor for something, Jane. No one can be that strong; everyone needs some help." It was the same advice I gave Joe so many months before. I'm pretty headstrong at times; I always insisted that I was fine. I could handle this.

Antidepressants and anti-anxiety medication weren't in my wheel-house or my family's. We were taught to be strong, to put our faith in God, and to take care of what needed to be done. And so I did. As long as there was hope, I had no reason to seek help; hope was my drug to get me through the tough days. But now there was no hope, and I didn't know what to do. I was looking at the days ahead, and I didn't know how I was going to face them—the inevitable wake, the funeral, the final goodbye.

I walked into the always-crowded family lounge. On this day, I wanted noise around me to drown out the conversation I was about to have. I found a corner in an out-of-the-way place and took out my cell phone. When Dr. Curran, my internist, answered, I told him I finally needed some help.

"Jane, I was wondering when you were going to call me."

I felt better just hearing his voice.

Joe hung on; he didn't want to leave me, us, everything he loved. The doctors were in and out constantly. Joe's blood pressure kept dropping; they couldn't sustain it no matter how much medication they gave him. It would rise, and then it would drop again. I was slowly losing him.

One day, one of the many cardiologists came by, checked on Joe, and then walked outside with me. "Mrs. Bavoso, I just don't understand why things like this happen to such nice people." It wasn't just my family who was feeling this pain; it was the whole transplant and cardiac team that had come to know Joe and our family so well over these many months.

That statement haunted me. Why do things like this happen to nice people? Why didn't God answer our prayers? Joe was a good man; he loved and took care of his family. He was honest and hardworking. Why didn't God step in and help him?

And then the answer came to me. I knew God didn't do this to Joe, because I believe in a caring and compassionate God. My belief is that God put us here to live our lives in the best way we can and to make our own decisions between right and wrong; sometimes bad things just happen. Maybe God judges us on the way we handle situations, but I don't believe

God changes anything. I think prayers make us feel better and comfort those we pray for.

I had a long conversation with an old friend one night, and she agreed with me. Her theory was that "God doesn't change anything, but He does cry with us." I found that statement to be beautiful.

I knew that God was crying with Joe every day, watching him suffer and struggle.

I also believed that when God finally beckoned Joe home, He would be so happy to welcome him but so very sad by the journey Joe had taken to get there.

CHAPTER TWENTY-EIGHT

THE FINAL GOODBYE

Lauren was sitting with me in my safe place when I saw Dr. Farr approaching. The look on her face told me she had nothing good to say. "Mrs. Bavoso, I know you realize that we can't get Joe better. We've tried everything, done everything medically possible for him, but he's just too weak, and the infections are too strong. His body can't fight any longer."

I knew what was coming, but I sat silently listening to this compassionate doctor who stole my husband's heart the first time he laid eyes on her. She was hurting as much as I was, and this conversation was not an easy one. I wondered whether she had pulled the short straw, if she found herself the unlucky loser to bring bad news to the family, but I doubted it. Knowing Dr. Farr, she probably took this upon herself because she had become so much a part of our lives.

After Joe received the second heart and was feeling so great in the hospital, he was making plans. That was Joe, always making plans. He was outlining, in a black marble notebook, the story he was going to write about this whole experience.

But he was also making plans for a celebratory dinner. He said, "When I'm strong again, I want to take Dave, Jenn, and Dr. Farr out to dinner. I might invite some others, but those three for sure. I have to thank them in some small way for all they did for me. Do you think they'd come? I think

I should be strong enough by March." And then he proceeded to look up restaurants, asking my opinion.

"We should go to a restaurant in Hoboken," Joe remarked.

"How come?" I asked.

"Because Dave and Dr. Farr live in the city, and Jenn lives in New Jersey. It would be easier for them." The man who just went through two heart transplants and lived on Long Island wanted to make it easier for the three people who helped him on his journey.

I smiled and answered, "I think that's a great idea."

Dr. Farr continued, this time with tears streaming down her face. "We can't keep his BP up. The medication isn't working, and there's nothing else we can do. Jane, I think Joe's in pain. He's grabbing the sheet every time his BP drops dangerously low. I can see the grimace on his face. I know he will never give up, but we can't help him anymore. This is a decision you and your family must make, but I think it's time to let him go. We'll make him comfortable; he'll experience no pain. But this is your decision."

I knew this was coming, but it was still a shock. I could hardly catch my breath. How could I make the decision to say goodbye to my husband, the love of my life, the boy I fell in love with before I was fifteen?

"My son needs to be here." That was the first thing I could think of to say.

"Of course," Dr. Farr answered. "If you like, I can come back tonight and discuss this with the three of you."

The decision was made. No more extraordinary means, no more raising his BP only to have it come crashing down again. But Joe was a fighter; I knew he wouldn't give up easily, no matter what. And so the vigil began.

During those days, numerous doctors who had cared for Joe over those many months stopped by, knowing I would be there. Their words of praise for this remarkable patient were nonstop. Dr. Tsiouris, the infectious disease doctor who we got to know so well, looked at me and said, "It was an honor and a privilege to have met and cared for your husband. He was a remarkable man. I will never forget him."

Dave stopped by, unaware of what was happening. When I informed him, he looked shocked. "You know, Dave, he loved you."

Dave looked at me and quietly said, "And I loved him."

The LVAD nurses came by, these talented young women who started this journey with Joe. They were speechless, the pain evident in their eyes, but they extended their arms for hugs—still wearing their blue GO JOE bracelets.

The ICU nurses who had taken such good care of Joe offered prayers for their favorite patient.

And then came the family. Joe's siblings, who had just buried a brother three and a half years before, came to say goodbye. I had no words as I watched them surround Joe's bed.

Finally came Pop, Joe's father, the patriarch of the family. At ninety-three, he was still one of the smartest and mentally alert men I knew. He had been praying and holding onto hope all these many months that God would spare his eldest son. The loss of Danny still weighed heavily on him.

I watched him as he slowly entered the room, accompanied by his youngest son. He walked around the bed and seated himself on a chair next to Joe. He picked up Joe's hand, held it, and lowered his head.

He sat still for a few minutes, either praying or saying goodbye. He then looked up at me and said, "You know, you're an angel."

"No," I replied, "I just love your son."

I couldn't leave Joe. I had been with him since this journey began, and I knew I had to be there when this journey was over. I never wanted him to feel alone or abandoned, so I decided to stay at the hospital that night. Lauren wouldn't let me stay alone. She kept me company, even though she had four small children at home.

No matter what history leads us to believe, women are the strongest creatures God ever created. We may not be able to lift a car or a pile of wood, but emotionally we can hold our own against any man. Peter opted to go home. I knew he couldn't bear this, and I was okay with it. I understood how painful this was for him, and I knew he couldn't watch his father fade away anymore. But, true to his nature, he ran around the hospital floor gathering sheets, pillows, and blankets. He returned to the room and put chairs together to make beds for Lauren and me. He was doing what he did best—trying to make us comfortable.

He would be back in the morning.

There was no sleep for either Lauren or me that night. In the morning, we left the hospital to go home for a few hours to shower, eat, and return by early afternoon.

Peter was there when we arrived. We sat with Joe as the hours ticked by. As evening approached, both Peter and Lauren turned to me and said, "Mom, you can't stay again tonight. This could go on for another week. You need to rest. You need to go home."

I knew they were right, but the thought of leaving Joe tore me apart. I gave in to their concern, but before I left, I stood by Joe's bed and held his hand.

It was dark. The lights were twinkling on the George Washington Bridge. Months ago, when there was still hope, I loved gazing at that bridge, watching the stream of cars going in and out of the city. But now I closed the shades; I was done looking at it. I had been looking out this window for eight months, and now all I could hear was the sound of the ventilator pushing breath in and out of Joe. The beeping of the machines told me that his blood pressure was dropping and the end was near.

I stood beside the bed and looked down at my once strong, virile husband and thought, *What do I do now? What is the proper procedure for watching someone die? Do I give him permission to leave, to go where there is no more pain?* It occurred to me that that's what every book on death instructs the family to do: "You must give the patient permission to die."

I didn't want to give Joe permission. I wanted to grab his shoulders and shake him; I wanted to tell him not to leave me, that I couldn't live without him. I wanted to scream at the top of my lungs that I wanted our life back. I wanted to remind him that we had lots of things to do. We had grandchildren to watch grow; we had faraway places to visit. We planned on growing old together. I wanted to beg him, don't leave me, please don't leave me.

But I didn't. I leaned over, kissed him on the cheek, and whispered in his ear. "Joe, I have loved you for most of my life. Thank you for the life you shared with me; thank you for being my protector, my hero, my champion. Thank you for creating our children with me. I know you want to stay, but you can't; you have fought as hard as you could. I will love you forever. But now you have to go."

CHAPTER TWENTY-NINE

The Days That Followed

Death Leaves a Heartache No One Can Heal,
Love Leaves a Memory No One Can Steal.
Anonymous

Update: Joe—Friday, June 18, 2010

Family and Friends,

*Our long journey is over. Joe passed away yesterday, June 17,
at 3:47 a.m. He fought the good fight and stayed true to himself
until the end. His body just could not sustain any more infections.*

That's how I began my final email update. Thinking back, I don't know
how I wrote it the day after I lost Joe, but I knew I had to tell our supporters and followers that the end had come. I described the last days and
the doctors and nurses who had come to say goodbye. I spoke of Joe's love
for family and friends. I spoke of Joe's love for me.

I ended with the following:

*I hope you will always remember Joe in some small way. Remember
him for his courage, strength, and love of life and family. Thank
you all for taking this journey with us; it helped us both during
these difficult months. Joe is at peace, and that gives me some
small amount of comfort.*

The hours after Joe's death were a blur. Marty called the funeral home in our town where everyone holds the wake or viewing for a loved one.

The four of us gathered around a large desk as the funeral director inquired as to our needs and wants. We knew that we needed two nights and the largest room. The family was big, the friends and acquaintances many.

The director pushed a book towards me. "Why don't you choose a prayer or inspirational verse for the memorial card?" he suggested. I knew he was trying to keep me busy. I wasn't concentrating on anything that he and my children were discussing. I remember thinking to myself, *It will take me forever to find something in this tome.* I opened the large book, turned about three pages, and there it was:

2 Timothy 4:7

I have fought the good fight, I have finished the course, I have kept my faith.

It was perfect.

Peter decided we should place some of Joe's photographs around the viewing room. "Let people see what a great photographer he was, Mom. Dad always wanted to do a one-man show anyway." And so we did.

We put Joe's large canvas photographs on easels and scattered them around the room. Peter suggested that we bring two boxes of Joe's 5x7 photos. They were placed by the podium where the guest book was open with a sign that read, "Please take a piece of Joe home with you. Choose a favorite photo."

We didn't expect many visitors the first day because it was Father's Day, but the room was filled to capacity, and there was a line of people waiting in the hall.

I felt a touch on my shoulder, and when I turned, I saw Drs. Marzo and Germano. I greeted them just as Joe would have, like old friends.

When the last visitors had left, I stood alone in the room, my heart aching, lost in my thoughts, wondering how I was going to manage to say my last goodbye, how I was going to live my life without my true companion by my side. I started to walk toward the back and saw Dave standing there with his fiancée, Valerie. I approached him with outstretched arms. "I was visiting my dad on Shelter Island for Father's Day, and I knew I had to come and say goodbye to Joe," Dave said to me.

I looked at Valerie, this young woman I had never met but heard so much about. Tears were streaming down her face. I was sure Dave had told her about his and Joe's special relationship.

The day of the service, as the funeral director was helping me out of the limo, he told me, "The church is packed with people." I wasn't surprised.

Father Dan, who was with us when we received the news of the second heart, officiated at the Mass at our request. He gave a beautiful homily, speaking of Joe and his faith. And then Peter got up to the podium and gave the eulogy. He spoke confidently and lovingly and ended with the words, "Go, Joe!"

As we were walking out of the church, a small hand slipped into mine. It was Jack, dressed in his somber black suit and tie. My little man had decided to escort his grandmother up the aisle.

We buried Joe in the small, historic Episcopalian cemetery directly across the street from our own parish church. He had taken many photos of the original wood-framed church that stood in the center of the graveyard, and because all Joe wanted was to come home, we decided to keep him as close to home as possible.

There was a large gathering at the burial site, and the funeral director quickly got a chair for Joe's father. I glanced over and noticed Jack scooting next to his great-grandfather and place his arm lovingly around Pop's shoulders. The oldest and one of the youngest in our family were grieving together. As people approached the casket, a few people placed their GO JOE bracelet on the coffin in lieu of a flower.

It was the final tribute to a life well lived.

Over the following days, my mother's words, spoken to me after the death of my father, resonated in my head. "And then everyone goes home to their life, and you're left alone with yours." I made a decision: I would accept any invitation from family or friends. No matter how I felt, I would not stay home and wallow.

I went on many field trips to the beach and park with Lauren and the four children. I traveled to New Jersey and spent time with Peter, Janine, Jack, and Julia.

I accepted invitations for a glass of wine and dinner from friends.

The local Artist's Association, of which Joe was a member, contacted me. They planned on honoring Joe at the outdoor art show that Joe had originally initiated. Peter, Lauren, and I were asked to be judges for the best photograph at the show. The Association would present an award in Joe's name. It was a moving moment for us all, and the event was written up in the local newspaper.

Memorials were written about Joe in his industry magazines. He had been a member of a few oil association boards, and I was informed that a moment of silence was held in Joe's memory before each meeting.

All of it was touching, but Peter, Lauren, and I knew there was something else we needed to do for Joe. We had to give him his one-man show. He had been talking about it before the heart transplant, planning on it being his first big event when he was healthy again. And so it began. I contacted the president of the Artist's Association. I didn't know this man, and he never met Joe. He had become a member during the time Joe was ill. He invited me to one of their monthly meetings to explain what I had in mind. This was not my thing. It's difficult for me to walk into a room of strangers and make a presentation. So I held my breath and hoped that Joe would guide me.

The room was full of friendly smiles. Some of them knew Joe, and some didn't. I explained what I wanted to do, bringing with me Joe's self-published book of his photos. The book was passed around, and the conversation was cordial. They agreed to host the event. I would be allowed to use the Artist

Circle Gallery to display and sell Joe's photographs. All proceeds would go to Joe's favorite charity, The Wounded Warriors.

The exhibit took place over the last weekend in September for three nights and two days. On opening night, we were filled to capacity with people standing outside waiting to enter. By Sunday night, every large canvas photograph that hung on the wall was sold. Most of the 8x10 and 5x7 photos were also gone.

The sale was a huge success, with the proceeds exceeding over $11,000 donated to Wounded Warriors.

On Sunday evening, as we were walking out the door of the gallery, Lauren turned to me, "Mom, look up." And there in the sky was the most beautiful rainbow. "Mom, Dad's happy," she said with a smile.

I had started to keep a journal after Joe's death. I needed to know whether I was progressing or regressing. It's good therapy for the mind and soul.

But there was something else I needed to do. I knew I had to write Joe's story. Some of the words in Peter's eulogy resounded in my head:

Dad showed me who we are in this family—

Fighters

Right until the end

Sure, it is quite possible that you will not win, but

That really has no bearing on the approach

It is simple

Fight the good fight. Push harder

Always want to win. Never doubt it can be done

I needed to let Joe's grandchildren know who they came from and what type of man he was. I needed to keep Joe's memory alive.

I mentioned this to a friend who was a writer. She had encouraged me to write after reading my updates that I sent out regularly during the many months of Joe's illness. She insisted that I attend a writing class with her at our local library. To this day, I don't know why I said yes. Maybe I was keeping the promise to myself to always accept an invitation. This was difficult for me. I had never written anything that was meant to be read by others, except for Joe's updates. I had no idea how to go about it, and knowing I had to read in front of an audience of eighteen to twenty people terrified me. But attend I did, and to this day I thank her for pushing me. I found a new love—writing—and so many encouraging, caring people. And so I told myself: "You have ten years, Jane, to learn how to write and put a book together."

CHAPTER THIRTY

THE DAYS BECOME YEARS

We lead our lives like water flowing down a hill,
going more or less in one direction until we
splash into something that forces us to find a new course.
Arthur Golden, *Memoirs of a Geisha*
June 17, 2020

It has been ten years since Joe's death.

I often think of the saying, "The days are long, but the years are short." Indeed, ten years ago, the days seemed very long. I questioned each one, wondering how I was going to get to the next day and the one after that. Before I knew it, a year had passed, and I had somehow survived. And then another day began, and another, and I now find myself here, a decade later. For Joe's tenth anniversary the family had planned on being together to share memories and celebrate his life, but the coronavirus pandemic prevented that. Lauren and I met at the cemetery and placed roses on his grave. I looked down at Joe's marker: Husband, Father, and Papa. His three greatest accomplishments.

"I'm okay, Joe," I told him. "Lots of things have happened."

I stood there reflecting on the past ten years.

I was told that life goes on. I couldn't imagine that in the beginning. If you allow it, loneliness creeps in quietly. It clutches you tightly and takes your breath away when you least expect it. It's your darkest enemy, depriving you of worth and hope. So I knew I had to make some memories of my own.

"October 2012 found me in Italy. I wasn't sure if I was ready to travel without you, but I did. I thought of you and all the wonderful photos you would have taken.

In the spring of 2014, I traveled to the British Isles. I knew you yearned to see Ireland and Scotland, so I went to see them for you.

The end of 2014 brought a major health crisis. It was the first time I faced anything so serious without you. Although I missed having you by my side, holding my hand and making me feel safe, I wasn't as frightened as I thought I should be. I knew you were with me, and if something happened, you would come and take me home. But I also knew I had things to finish here on earth—my job wasn't done. Those thoughts gave me the courage to get through some tough days.

In 2016 I visited Charleston and Savannah. I loved Charleston the second time as much as I did the first time, when we explored the city together.

2017 brought my seventieth birthday. Because you weren't here to plan and surprise me with something special as I know you would have, I decided to hatch a plan myself. I took the family to Beaches in Turks and Caicos. I missed sharing with you the experience of watching the kids frolic in the water, diving off a raft, snorkeling, and having fun and laughing together.

In 2018 I traveled to Alaska. Again, I took many photos, trying to see through the lens as you would.

October 2019 found me in Paris. Five days of walking for miles, sipping champagne at outdoor cafes, and strolling the streets of the Champs-Elysees. I know you never wanted to see Paris, but it really is a gorgeous city.

The years have been busy, Joe, recalling old memories and making new ones.

Your babies are doing well and growing up quickly. We now have five teenagers and one pre-teen. Jack is a talented artist. He takes after your side of the family. Julia is musical. She's teaching herself the guitar and is involved in community theatre. Kieran, our scholar, is still focused on his future. Luke is your fisherman. He's never happier than when he's on a boat with a rod in his hand or swimming under the water, observing sea life. Nora is a leader. She makes decisions on what's best for her, not what her friends think. Hannah, the one you held in your arms for hours, is an independent thinker. Although always funny with a quick wit, she questions social issues and injustices.

You would be so proud of all of them. I've learned that life does go on—differently, maybe, but it forges ahead.

We have two choices: hop on and take the ride, or stand still and let the world go by. I made the decision to hop on and hold on tight."

My mind returned to the present as Lauren and I walked away from Joe's grave; I turned back for a moment and told him one last thing.

"Joe, guess what? Your story is finished. The book is complete. I kept my promise."